SOLVING
AND FLEXIBILITY PUZZLE

For Eileen and Steve,
with warmest regards.

Thank you, Eileen,
for giving your copy to
Ellen, and for your very
welcome support of my
struggling effort to tell
a thoughtful research story.

and, Steve, with
hopes that curiosity
will drive you to
read it as well,
without killing the cat.
I would value your
opinion.

P.S. This is one of those first
printing copies, with back cover errors,
item to keep you hale and hearty.

SOLVING THE CHILDCARE AND FLEXIBILITY PUZZLE

How Working Parents Make the Best Feasible Choices and What That Means for Public Policy

ARTHUR C. EMLEN

Universal-Publishers
Boca Raton

Solving the Childcare and Flexibility Puzzle: How Working Parents Make the Best Feasible Choices and What That Means for Public Policy

Universal-Publishers
Boca Raton, Florida • USA
2010

ISBN-10: 1-59942-868-7
ISBN-13: 978-1-59942-868-0

www.universal-publishers.com

Library of Congress Cataloging-in-Publication Data

Emlen, Arthur.
Solving the childcare and flexibility puzzle : how working parents make the best feasible choices and what that means for public policy / Arthur C. Emlen.
    p. cm.
Includes bibliographical references.
ISBN-13: 978-1-59942-868-0 (pbk. : alk. paper)
ISBN-10: 1-59942-868-7 (pbk. : alk. paper)
    1. Children of working parents--United States. 2. Child care--Government policy--United States. I. Title.
HQ777.6.E45 2010
362.71'20973--dc22
                                        2010001502

CONTENTS

PREFACE... VII

CHAPTER 1
The Big Picture.. 13

CHAPTER 2
The Achilles' Heel of a Worthy Profession 21

CHAPTER 3
Parents Have Their Reasons 29

CHAPTER 4
The Sources of Flexibility.. 39

CHAPTER 5
Measuring Quality of Care and Flexibility.................. 51

CHAPTER 6
The Flexibility Solution.. 61

CHAPTER 7
Flexibility and Quality of Care.................................... 67

CHAPTER 8
An Explanatory Hypothesis.. 73

CHAPTER 9
A New Direction In Public Policy 81

CHAPTER 10
Solving the Flexibility Puzzle 103

ACKNOWLEDGMENTS 109
WORKS CITED... 115
ABOUT THE AUTHOR.. 121

PREFACE

"Go to nature, take the facts into your own hands,
look, and see for yourself."

~Louis Agassiz as recalled by William James[1]

Whatever happened to daycare in the United States? And why is that an intriguing question? An answer requires us to look beneath the surface of three disconnected worlds: the parents' world, the profession of early childhood care and education, and the politics of daycare.

If you stop and listen in on the politics of daycare, the scene seems strangely quiet. Did you ever hear the subject mentioned in the last two or three presidential campaigns? Neither party knew what to say about childcare or even about the survival of American families, though these matters are of daily concern to millions. Were the priorities too low? Was the subject too dull, too complex, the answers too simple? Yes, maybe, to all those reasons, but there is another. The policy positions and political agendas coming from advocates of opposite persuasion had no resonance. All you could hear was the hush of political stalemate.

I think I can explain how it happened. The stalemate was triggered by fearful reactions to tumultuous economic and social change and to the philosophy and policy agenda of a vanguard of child-care

---

[1] My source was Lyanda Haupt, *Crow Planet: Essential Wisdom from the Urban Wilderness* (Little, Brown and Company, 2009), p.143.

advocates. Worthy people devoted to children and their development made a tragic error in how they sought to professionalize daycare. The caregivers of this world deserve our appreciation, and their work needs no justification at the expense of parents. But that is what happened. An emerging profession that never liked the daycare arrangements parents were making dreamed instead of a sweeping system of professional-quality childcare. It is an ironic history of concern for children, blame for parents, and an all-consuming pursuit of quality childcare, a Holy Grail blinding in its appeal. Although the profession never achieved its goal of a universally subsidized system of professional-quality care, it stayed narrowly focused on training providers of childcare and creating islands of quality in a vast sea of daycare.

It left the parents behind. The larger world is the one where parents live and families struggle, where tattered safety nets fail and families go bankrupt, where tens of millions of employed parents are either two-earner couples or single, where parents make difficult decisions and perform feats of flexibility as they work full-time or part-time or stay home, rely on grandmother, or search for something in the marketplace.

How do parents manage all that? This book has a research story to tell about the dynamics of how parents make these challenging decisions, and of how they triumph over adverse circumstances, if they can, by mobilizing diverse sources of flexibility within their lives. Turns out, they do that to good effect. Their discriminating ability will earn your respect and surprise you if you have too easily been impressed by decades of negative opinion about parents.

Does it really matter what we believe about parents? It does if parents got a bum rap that was used to justify bad policy. It does if America's childcare problem is diagnosed as parents making poor choices due to incompetence or weak motivation to choose quality of care, and if that diagnosis is used to justify a policy agenda that does not respect parental choice.

On the other hand, if careful critique debunks that line of argument and if new research presents contrary evidence and offers a compelling positive explanation of how parents make decisions about the choices open to them, then we have alternative propositions that are incompatible. What we believe has consequences pivotal for the direction policy will take. By revising our understanding of parents' circumstances and behavior we can re-think policy about families, employment, and childcare. We can break the stalemate that pits support for childcare against support for the wellbeing of families.

The heart of this treatise documents the ability of parents to make sound decisions about employment and childcare. I describe research evidence that explains the dynamics of this remarkable ability. My conclusions would not be so surprising were it not for the strange history of an emerging childcare profession that in its earnest pursuit of professional-quality became convinced that parents have poor judgment and make poor arrangements. Dismissive of parental choice, the profession developed a social philosophy that quite left families out of the picture. I chronicle the attitude and the faulty inferences that led the profession astray.

I call it a strange history, because it seems clear to me favorable outcomes for children cannot by achieved simply by improving childcare. The scope of that effort is too limited. It is a childcare policy without a family policy. It leaves out efforts to strengthen the financial security of families and the working conditions of parents. It ignores the great variety of social arrangements that families make inside or outside the home. In other words, it ignores the immediate environment that shapes which childcare choices will be feasible.

This treatise fills a gap. It explains why parents make the best childcare arrangements that are possible for them to make. The amount of flexibility that parents can squeeze out of their immediate environment—from work schedules, shared family responsibility, and supportive childcare—is the key to better choices of childcare. This research documents how parents come up with their own distinctive *flexibility solution* that makes the best choice possible—and more likely.

How did I come to write this? How did I come by this point of view? I trace the origins of my interest in these matters back 44 years when I had an opportunity to provide research consultation to a neighborhood project that was figuring out how to gather a network of supportive women who knew their neighbors and could help working mothers find daycare in family homes. These parents and caregivers were discovering each other and creating a new, informal market in "family daycare." I was gripped with curiosity. Son of an ornithologist, I grew up among naturalists. So it was no stretch for me to be studying employed parents and their daycare with all the objectivity and naturalistic wonder one might apply to observing the nesting behavior of birds. I wondered how satisfied they were with these arrangements, and I wanted to know why some lasted a long time while others were of brief duration?

At the same time, I began noticing that the professional community strongly disapproved of these childcare arrangements made informally in the neighborhood. I became curious about that too. I wondered why national agencies shunned a natural phenomenon that would have been heralded as a success had it been an organized program—either government or corporate. Instead, they called it a form of "neglect."

The sharp discrepancy between parent behavior and the professional response to it drew my attention as an issue in itself. In the politics of daycare, I was hearing the first notes of an attitude I would hear repeated over and over with increasing intensity and articulation. It was a theme discordant with what I would learn about parents over a career of studying how parents manage to deal with employment, family, and childcare. I draw on much of that experience for this book, which tries to understand those disparate worlds.

Altogether, in addition to spending several years studying family daycare, interviewing working mothers and their neighborhood caregivers over the duration of their arrangement together, I also conducted employee surveys for employers. I surveyed more than 50,000 employees from 124 companies in 25 cities and 13 states. For the state of Oregon, I surveyed low-income parents receiving childcare assistance, and I conducted statewide market-rate surveys of childcare prices. I surveyed representative Oregon households in a biennial survey. And I led a study to measure quality of childcare from a parent's point of view and to understand the conditions associated with it.

I worked closely with practitioners, professionals, administrators and other researchers in the field of childcare, and I developed great respect for them and their work. Such a group assembled in 1989 as a "data group" to develop information that could drive statewide childcare policy. I was a charter member of that group, which initially met in our kitchen, and we have met monthly ever since—for the past 20 years. After six years, the data group became the Oregon Child-Care Research Partnership—a virtual organization, belonging to no other for many years. It has stimulated numerous funded research projects involving a network of agencies, and holds an annual roundtable on timely issues.

The auspices for my own research have been academic. At Portland State University, I taught research methods and child welfare at the Graduate School of Social Work, and for 17 years directed the Regional Research Institute for Human Services. When I became an emeritus professor, I started my own company to continue employee surveys for several years, and then returned to the university to conduct the quality-of-care study.

While my association with the childcare profession has been collaborative, as was my work with employers on work-family issues, most of my research has been looking closely at how employed parents manage. My interest in quality of care was to study it, and to measure it, from a parent's point of view. And at every stage of my career, what I learned about parents was contrary to a negative bias that seemed to have infected much of professional thinking, research, and advocacy.

Starting crudely, that attitude towards parents began with disparagement of their arrangements, moved to discrediting their judgment, and ended in uncritical belief in idealized measures of childcare quality. Evaluative ratings were reported as science and became national facts. The early theme became symphonic. In a crescendo of blame, expert opinion used attitude and faulty findings to draw a caricature of parents that justified leaving them behind.

For me, a telling example occurred in 1995 at Oregon's first annual childcare researchers' roundtable, when I was describing how we would measure quality of childcare from a parent's point of view. An early childhood specialist, whose Ph.D. was in developmental psychology, challenged me, "We already know what quality of care is. Why ask parents?" I took that as a question, but it was really a statement that the whole idea was preposterous—that "we" know better, and asking parents is unnecessary.

This attitude, I fear, is the profession's Achilles heel—destined to be its undoing—unless it starts to take parents seriously and begins to take the diversity of family needs and values into account. I am not criticizing what childcare professionals do in their work. Many of them are my colleagues and friends who do care about parents. My criticism is directed at attitudes and beliefs that have become prevalent within their profession, that have escaped refutation so far, and that restrict the scope of professional concerns and efforts. I think of this critique as a plea to an otherwise worthy profession.

Why do they have such an unrealistic policy agenda? Why should professionals hold a negative attitude towards parents with such persistence? Is it true, what they keep saying about parents? How *do* parents decide which childcare arrangements make sense for them? What does drive their choices? And how would national policy be different, if parental judgment were respected and if families were strongly supported in their economic security and capacity to manage?

I call this a "treatise" because the format is of unfolding logic that spells out evidence, inferences, and conclusions drawn. Academically, it is about the ecology of human behavior—specifically about parental judgment when parents make decisions about childcare. Those decisions take place in a natural environment and are shaped by the constraints and resources of geography, neighborhood, work, and family, as well as by the childcare market and any childcare a community may provide.

I offer my thanks to many for their assistance and encouragement. My acknowledgments are rather long because I am indebted to so many over the years. They appear at the end.

Chapter 1

The Big Picture

"The big picture that emerges suggests it's high time for an era of empowered child-care consumerism."

~Sue Shellenbarger, *Work & Family: Essays from the "Work & Family" Column of The Wall Street Journal* [2]

The big daycare picture is of three discordant worlds, ignorant of each other, unheeding, in unharmonious pursuit of competing solutions. Throughout a decades-long history, daycare has been seen through a narrow and distorted lens that left families out of the picture. Although public policy largely depends upon families to manage as best they can, their work and family interests have been slighted, and their economic capacity to manage well has been ignored. The new profession devoted to the childcare, education, and development of children had eyes only for childcare solutions. Concerned about the daycare arrangements many parents were making, and blaming the problem on failures of parental behavior, the profession sought to supplant existing arrangements with a subsidized system of professional-quality childcare.

Political stalemate. Advocacy of that far-reaching solution, however, provoked apprehension in varied sectors, as laissez-faire libertarians weighed in against the "nanny state" (Olsen 1997), and advocates of "family values" opposed commercial daycare (Robertson 2003). The reaction is reminiscent of the standoff almost four decades ago, when President Nixon vetoed the Child Care and Child

---

[2] (New York: Ballantine Books, 1999), p. 17.

Development Act of 1971. That bill tried to create a comprehensive system of childcare services with a strong center-care bias. Its advocates have not understood the drawbacks of that legislation—then or since.

Since then, the profession's dream has continued to meet with wide resistance, never attracting political support from either political party—and not just because of the cost. Universal childcare was not a featured issue in any presidential campaign. The national debate has not occurred. The net result of extreme proposal and extreme reaction—listened to only within separate enclaves—was a prolonged stalemate in public policy. Avoiding comprehensive childcare, on the one hand, and distracting national attention from the health and economic strength of families, on the other, official policy has remained narrowly focused on improving the "supply" of childcare for low-income children.

The state of national policy. This meant regulatory standards for the health, safety, and staffing of childcare. Especially—and with passion—it meant promoting professional training for the childcare workforce. In addition to very modest tax exemptions per parent and per child, it also meant some public subsidy for the use of childcare—through tax credits on a sliding scale for many parents who have some choice about their hours of childcare and employment. For low-income families it meant food stamps and school lunches and some assistance to states for health insurance. For those receiving public assistance, it meant a time-limited period of government-paid care. For those parents, however, policy required longer hours of work and childcare, even though their children were younger. For a low-income population, public policy also meant Head Start—a fully-supported preschool and child-development program with health services and parent involvement. Though it was primarily a half-day, center-based program serving nearly a quarter and eventually half of its eligible low-income population, Head Start enjoyed political support from a strong constituency and probably came the closest of any public policy to the profession's dream of providing a model for universal childcare.

Nevertheless, that vision was far from realized. Despite a mixture of federal, state, community, and corporate expenditures, families continue to provide most of the financing of childcare. Community-based "resource and referral" services assist the market for out-of-home childcare, but parents—well-informed or not—continue to make the decisions—about good choices or not.

How were families managing? In the unseen world of family life, the histories of maternal employment and daycare are intertwined. Driven by powerful economic forces and social movements, this is a history of upheaval that brought opportunities and achievements, as well as anxiety over the changes in work, childcare, and family life. Families sought ways to make new social arrangements. With new kinds of jobs, new forms of family care emerged and new daycare markets developed, resulting in wide diversity in patterns of childcare.

To the changing economic and social challenges, families responded in a myriad of different ways that fit their circumstances, met their needs, and reflected their values. Many employed couples split shifts to avoid use of daycare. For help with childcare, many turned to grandmothers. Others discovered an unrelated caregiver among stay-at-home mothers nearby in the neighborhood. Within family homes, silently and unheralded, a new daycare market emerged, as maternal employment became a way of life for a majority even of young families.

Over the decades, childcare centers attracted an increasing share of the overall market, but the dominant characteristic of the family picture today remains a wide diversity in types of care. Whether for single parents or dual earners, or for families with one parent staying at home, myriad choices are made: full or part-time employment, daycare or no daycare, reliance on relative or non-relative, paid care or unpaid, care at home or out-of-home in a center or a family home, or any combination of multiple arrangements. This diversity in the kinds of arrangements that families are making reflects their varied circumstances, as well as differences in personal values.

The diversity of childcare in the United States is well documented. When we talk about "childcare," what do we mean? A 1997 survey (Smith 1997) shown in Table 1.1 takes a broad view, with a scope that encompasses 100 percent of all arrangements made by *employed* mothers in the United States—and by fathers in households where there is no mother—for 100 percent of all of their children who are under the age of 15. This is not the most recent national survey, but shifts in market share do not change the big picture.

This is not all of the children or arrangements in the United States, of course—approximately 30 percent of children in families in which the mother is *not* employed also use childcare and related activities for other purposes, such as education, volunteer work, respite, or offering their child some good experiences outside the home.

However, it is useful to focus on the arrangements of *employed* mothers, plus of the solo fathers. Some might object that any parental care is properly classified as child rearing not as "caregiving," but this table provides a more complete perspective on the arrangements made for children when maternal employment is involved.

Table 1.1. Employed Mothers' Arrangements for Preschoolers Under 5 and for School-Age Children 5-14

Source: "Who's Minding the Kids? Child Care Arrangements: Spring 1997. Current Population Reports, U.S. Census Bureau, Survey of Income and Program Participation (SIPP) 1996 Panel Wave 4 Conducted between April and July 1997.

Percent of Children of Employed Mothers

Arrangement	Children Under 5	Children 5-14
Relative home care (child's or relative's home)		
Mother	5.1	4.9
Father	30.6	26.2
Grandparent	29.6	19.3
Sibling or other relative	14.8	21.0
In child's home		
Non-relative home care		
In child's home	5.5	4.6
In provider's home (family daycare)	22.8	10.0
Organized care facility		
Daycare center	18.9	8.5
Nursery or preschool	7.0	
Head Start, kindergarten, or school	3.4	
Enrichment activity		20.9
Self care		84.7
In multiple arrangements not school or self	30.2	25.7
Number of children of employed mothers	10,116,000	23,423,000
Number of all children*	19,611,000	39,486,000
* includes children living with fathers	417,000	1,461,000
Percent of all children who live with an employed mother or with father	51.6	59.3

This table does not try to pick the "primary arrangement" that families use most, but reports multiple arrangements instead. The types of primary arrangements would be mutually exclusive and would add up to 100 percent, but since many families make multiple arrangements, valuable information would be lost. Rather than lose that information, Table 1.1 brings out the true diversity of supplemental use of childcare by reporting the percentage of the *children* of employed mothers (plus children with fathers only). These numbers add up to more than 100 percent and indicate the extent to which parents use multiple arrangements. Multiple arrangements are criticized by advocates of full-day childcare, but they create options that make a lot of sense for families. Table 1.1 is divided into two parts: preschoolers under 5 and school-age children 5-14.[3] Approximately half of U.S. preschool children and 6 out of 10 school-age children have an employed mother. Of those children, about half are in daycare arrangements involving their father or a grandparent; and other relatives are also important. As you can see, it takes a diversity of arrangements. Examine Table 1.1 for details. Over time, although centers have been increasing their share of the out-of-home childcare market, the big picture is this diversity of arrangements just described.

The diversity of arrangements is most obviously associated with differences in who is providing the care and where it is located, such as in a family home or an organized center. Equally important, though, is how the arrangements are made. Arrangements with grandmothers, other relatives, friends, and some neighbors grow out of prior, established relationships. If not already close and trusted, these caregivers are at least a known member of a kinship network or time-honored association in the neighborhood. A parent has direct personal knowledge of this person, and the caregiver is motivated to help out this particular mother or take care of this particular child. These arrangements are sometimes referred to as childcare by kith and kin. You don't have to search for them. The arrangements have to be negotiated, but they arise uniquely from familiar associations. They may involve paid care or not, but are probably not affected much by market rates. They tend be private and invisible to public agencies, except when reimbursed for childcare assistance.

Then there are arrangements parents must search for beyond kith and kin. In one sub-category of these situations, parents rely on information supplied by friends or neighborhood contacts who can vouch for a home caregiver or daycare center. This informal social

---

[3] Table 1.1 excludes 5-year olds, because school-age patterns of care are blurred somewhat by variation across states in the kindergarten opportunities of 5-year olds.

network provides an entrée and word-of-mouth assessment.[4] In a second sub-category of searched-for arrangements, parents contact an agency such as a childcare resource and referral service that can provide possible leads and assist in referral, but is chary about offering recommendations. The rest of the search is up to the parent. This second sub-category is the most clearly visible as part of an organized market. These home or center-based caregivers advertise, hang out their shingle, and post their prices. They are in the business and regularly take more than one or two children. There is public evidence of competition. Some of those in the business of childcare are profitable corporations with stockholders.

There is another mode of arrangement that probably does not involve a search. In these cases, the parent may be, or may become, a member of a church or a Head Start community, a client of an agency, or an employee eligible for a corporate childcare center. These services are established as a public good, often to demonstrate or provide a child development program of high quality, and the parent's childcare may be subsidized wholly or in part.

The differences among arrangements procured through prior association, a neighborhood network, a market search, or public-good services should not obscure what all of them have in common. Whether within or outside of a market, whether they involve an exchange of money for services, a bartering of gifts, or some social reciprocity, all of these arrangements are of economic importance to the family. Even though all of the options are not open to all, they all are choices within the market or alternatives to it. All family decisions about what kind of childcare to use, and how much, are intertwined with decisions about who will be employed, and how much.

The whole picture is a complex interplay of social, cultural, and economic relationships. All childcare choices are rooted in cultural values held by the family and shared by others. All depend on associations and personal relationships inside and outside the family, and in the neighborhood or wider community. All arrangements have strengths and drawbacks. They all vary in quality, and all of them may serve a valid purpose at a particular time in the life of a child, or in a stage of development of the family. All arrangements are subject to a parent's choice.

---

[4] Stanford economist John McMillan's *Reinventing the Bazaar: A Natural History of Markets* is a useful book in thinking about markets.

That is the big picture. It captures the great diversity of ways that working parents make arrangements for their families. Clashing with the big picture, however, is the direction taken by the childcare profession. That is described in the following chapter, along with a critique of how the profession went astray. Then we will resume the walking tour of the wider world in which families live and provide a realistic account of how parents actually make their decisions about employment and childcare. It will take several chapters to present evidence in support of a series of propositions, which, taken together, lead to a hypothesis that provides a satisfying explanation of these parental choices. This new understanding of parental behavior points in a new direction for public policy. The wellsprings of flexibility that support parental choice are to be found in policies that can strengthen families and the workplace, as well as childcare.

CHAPTER 2

THE ACHILLES' HEEL OF A WORTHY PROFESSION

"Lack of understanding of human nature is the
primary cause of disregard for it."

~John Dewey, *Human Nature and Conduct* [5]

Meanwhile, as families struggled, an emerging profession
that was devoted to the childcare, education, and development of young children, was concerned about the daycare arrangements that many parents were making. Instead of those
arrangements, they would create a trained, professional-quality childcare workforce and ensure more favorable outcomes for children in
out-of-home care. That would be society's answer to "America's
daycare problem."

But that vision was destined to fail. It was based on a fatal
flaw—an attitude that led the profession down a path sharply diverg-
ing from the paths families were taking. Instead of paying close and
respectful attention to how family circumstances and values were
shaping parental decisions, the profession became increasingly critical and dismissive of the ability of parents to make sound daycare
choices. For decades this disparaging attitude has followed parents
like a black cloud and has led to misguided childcare policy.

To understand how a worthy profession allowed itself to be led
astray, we must examine the origins and development of this attitude.
A step-by-step account of flawed evidence and faulty conclusions

---

[5] (New York: Henry Holt and Company, 1922), p. 3.

will show how a persistent negative prejudice developed into a social philosophy about childcare that became the profession's Achilles' heel.

Maternal employment and Sally Sly: Origins of an attitude. The attitude began with early concerns about maternal employment, even before the numbers of working mothers were large, before many turned to the daycare markets, or before the childcare profession had emerged. The attitude is illustrated by a children's book written 90 years ago by Thornton Burgess (1919). He described an indignation meeting in the Old Orchard when Sally Sly, the Cowbird, instead of making a nest of her own, laid her egg in the nest of Chebek, the Least Fly-catcher. Jenny Wren, the Old Orchard's chief scold, ranted about the behavior of that selfish good-for-nothing mother Sally Sly. Peter Rabbit's quiet efforts to understand what was going on failed to quiet the disturbance, and Jenny Wren's attitude is still with us today in some quarters.

Charges of neglect. Blaming parents for their daycare began in earnest in the 1960s and 70s, when maternal employment was no longer such an oddity. According to a national census (Low 1968), 20 percent of the children under 6 whose parents were employed full time, received care in out-of-home arrangements with caregivers who were not relatives. The establishment was not happy about that and referred to such care as a form of "neglect," first in a 1968 "Fact Sheet" from the Day Care and Child Development Council of America. Then, the U.S. Women's Bureau, again making the same whole-sale implication of "Neglect," estimated the number of daycare "slots" needed in the United States (Rosenberg 1969), simply by counting all of the 10.5 million children who were not in licensed or regulated care and asserting that number as the size of the population "in need" of childcare (Emlen 1970, 1972). They cited those statistics as the "Facts about Day Care." At that time, only 8 percent of the children were in organized group-care in childcare centers, and 72 percent were cared for either at home or by kin.

That grandmothers and other relatives were a source of childcare was well known, but authorities had difficulty accepting the idea that the parents of approximately two million children could, without any agency sponsorship, have successfully reached beyond family and kin to find "family daycare" in the neighborhood. The new market didn't always work perfectly, but it was a remarkable economic, social, and cultural invention. Had it been an organized program—public or private—it would have been called a success.

Care in family homes was viewed with suspicion and prejudice, however. In 1972, a study called *Windows on Day Care* (Keyserling 1972), rich in observation and bad sampling, featured horror stories, such as one about a licensed center with 47 children. The center's licensing, of course, was not enforced, but they called it a "family daycare home," to bolster their grossly biased generalization.

In a study in Portland, Oregon, conducted before any regulation of family homes, the neighborhood caregivers typically presented a very different picture. Taking in six or more children was a rare event. Of children under six years of age, typically she had one child of her own and added two more from other families, keeping well under any licensing limit a state might have imposed (Emlen 1971).

A new profession defines its mission. Gradually childcare advocates began to concentrate on development of a profession, featuring recruitment, training, career ladders, and certification. "I'm not just a babysitter" became a favorite slogan, as the profession defined itself as a provider of education, not just childcare, and took pains to call itself *childcare and early education.*

The discovery of "quality of care." In developing professional standards, educators and researchers devoted an impressive amount of effort to the task of defining and measuring the quality of care provided within a childcare setting. The *quality-rating scale* was born, first constructed by Thelma Harms and her colleagues for children in preschool programs (1980) and later for infants and toddlers in center care (1990), as well as for children in family daycare homes (1989). The Quality Rating Scale would capture a strong following within the profession. The first one, known as the ECERS, consisted of 37 evaluative ratings, made by trained observers, of the many facets of childcare activity. Points on a scale from 1 to 7 were anchored by descriptive categories ranging from poor or inadequate care to excellent care representing best professional practice.

Thus the measurement method converted descriptive observations into evaluative ratings expressed in value-laden language. In the final product, the descriptions were lost from sight, but the evaluations survived. The "findings" became "fact," and the evaluative judgments became "true," when in reality they were expressing degrees of departure from ideal standards. With seeming scientific authority, the results exaggerated the prevalence of childcare problems—though to an unknown degree. Uncritical belief in the validity of the quality rating scale involved a fundamental confusion.

Although the quality-rating-scale methodology and findings were faulty, the fault lies not with the legitimacy of evaluation, but with the way that values were allowed to confound the science. Evaluation is a fundamental and universal human ability. As a guide to action, we compare things to our values and standards. But we rely upon other human abilities—perception and cognition—to provide objective knowledge of the world we live in—to observe, supply the logic, and create the building blocks of science. Our values may direct our interest in what to study, but in building knowledge, we try to keep our values from infecting our judgments about what is objectively true and factual. When that resolve is lost and the lines blurred, we travel down a slippery slope, believing what we wish. And that is what happened with these rating scales measuring childcare quality.

Mediocre or worse. Use of the quality rating scale was in full force in a national study. Based on findings from the *Cost, Quality, and Child Outcomes Study,* 86 percent of childcare for children in 401 centers was found to be "mediocre" or worse (Helburn 1995). This allowed the profession to define "America's child care problem" as the overwhelming prevalence of substandard quality in the nation's childcare (Helburn 2002, 1995).

A shocking discrepancy between professional and parental judgment. In that same study, the investigators also obtained quality ratings from the parents (Cryer 1997; Cryer 1994; Helburn 1995), and they found a large discrepancy between professional and parental assessments. Not only did they find that the childcare is mediocre or worse, but that parents don't think so. Parents were deemed unable to discriminate known levels of quality accurately, partly for lack of information, access, and ability to observe, and for lack of knowledge of the ingredients of quality of care (Cryer 1997). A host of interpretations flew about, most of them psychological. Whether in a state of denial, or through resolution of "cognitive dissonance", or from generically dismissing the untrustworthiness of "self report", parents could now be thought to delude themselves about the poor choices they had made. A May 12, 1997 feature story in *U.S. News and World Report* described those research findings as *The Lies Parents Tell.* The sorry state of childcare sold well to the media, became widely believed by early childhood professionals (Kagen 1997), and in the 1997 White House Conference on Child Care, those featured "facts" became a national conclusion.

Misinterpretation and scientific contagion. How was it possible to overlook the methodological flaws on which the invidious comparison was based, using methods that were not comparable? One measure was complex and detailed, the other cursory. One measured deviation from an idealized standard of practice serving a group of children, the other ignored the parent's perspective with its more individualized assessment of the needs of the parent's own child. How was it possible not to recognize how exaggerated the finding of discrepancy really was? The exaggeration combined a professional assessment biased in a negative direction, with a parental rating biased in a positive direction. The combined effect of the exaggerations went unnoticed. In this climate of opinion it was easier to indulge in disparaging interpretations of parental behavior.

Use of the quality rating scale was part of a contagious boom in research into the quality of childcare, and the quality ratings appeared to have been confirmed by a body of research that was better grounded by empirical evidence. Investigators also examined quality of care in settings other than centers, such as in family homes and care by relatives (Galinsky 1994). A study of family daycare reported only 9 percent providing good quality care (Kontos 1995), and two-thirds of relatives offering inadequate quality (Kontos 1995). Investigators discovered important characteristics of care in childcare settings—such as the number of children in a group the ratio of children to adults, the training of staff, and the relationships between children and their caregivers—all of which were "quality indicators" associated with favorable outcomes for children. Developmental psychologists found evidence that professional-quality childcare has favorable consequences for those children who experience it, while "poor" quality care, and cumulative long hours of non-parental care, has adverse behavioral effects (NICHD 2006; Vandell 2001).

The central problem with this body of research, however, was not with the kernels of truth revealed by low but statistically significant correlation with quality ratings. The problem was the adoption of a common evaluative language and interpretation that, based on idealized standards, inherently exaggerated the realities of concern to an unknown degree, while focusing on findings of limited relevance to the larger picture of childcare in the context of parental and family life.

The modest relevance of the quality variables is illustrated by another kernel of truth that came from the same NICHD study—which is the most comprehensive study of child outcomes so far. Placing the childcare effects in a broader perspective, the study found substantially more powerful effects attributable to parenting and family variables, including maternal mental health.

Yet the profession persists in paying a lop-sided amount of attention to the childcare variables, spurred by preoccupation with the quality ratings. Although based on expensive use of professionally-trained observers, the quality ratings became so popular, they became an industry. They are still used in many states to promote high quality practice (Bureau 2007), although doubts are beginning to surface among some professionals.

Market failure attributed to an alleged weak demand for quality. Blaming parents reached a whole new level of sophistication when three economists gave new meaning to the quality-rating data from the cost and quality study cited above. John Morris (1999) theorized that consumer ignorance and "overestimation" of care quality rendered a market for quality of care impossible. David Blau (2001) argued that "The main problem in the childcare market is low quality. Childcare quality is low on average because the market responds to the demands of consumers, and the average consumer demands low-quality care. That is, the average consumer is unwilling to pay enough for high quality to cover the cost of providing it" (p. 11).

How did Blau reach that conclusion? He simply plugged into his econometric analysis the only data available—the quality-rating data. He recognized where his assumptions came from, and he is a stout defender of parental choice of childcare. But his work lent credibility to the thesis that America's childcare problem is one of "market failure," a view adopted by economist Suzanne Helburn (2002), in which the short supply of professionally-trained providers is attributed to weak demand for quality, as undiscriminating parents use a variety of childcare arrangements of lower quality.

Clearly, to question the wisdom of parents for not choosing a resource that is in short supply—largely unavailable and unaffordable to them—is an astonishing contradiction. Nevertheless, the professional diagnosis claimed that parents make poor choices because they are poorly informed about childcare quality, lack the ability to assess it, and do not place high value on it—a lack, not just of ability, but of motivation.

Parents selfishly sacrifice quality for personal convenience. Blaming Sally Sly recurred in the form of a more sophisticated argument. Early-childhood investigators created a dichotomy between kinds of childcare, based on whose interests are being served: "custodial," which is parent-oriented, vs. "developmental," which is child-oriented. "The choice of provider must satisfy two sets of often contradictory needs—the needs of the child and the needs of the parents" (Helburn 2002). With this frequently voiced assumption, all of the practical needs that parents have when they are choosing and arranging childcare—their need for convenience, proximity, affordability, and flexibility—are thought of as self-centered or selfish alternatives to the pursuit of quality childcare. Parents are thought to make a *trade off*, sacrificing quality of childcare for flexibility and personal convenience.

This presumption sounds so plausible to those who share that point of view, that the assertion was accepted as established fact. It is, however, a testable proposition. If it is really true that parents choose flexibility at the expense of quality, then research will find the two variables in conflict—inversely related—so the greater the flexibility that parents acquire, the worse the quality of care. The next chapters describe research that contradicts that proposition. Contrary to popular belief, the data reveal that flexibility plays a positive role in choice of childcare.

In summary, the childcare profession developed a world view consisting of the following assumptions and assertions:

1. Quality rating scales produce valid, factual findings.
2. Professional assessments prove that the quality of childcare in the United States is mostly mediocre or poor.
3. Low quality of care is attributable to low demand for quality by parents.
4. The discrepancy between parental and professional ratings proves that parents are unable to assess the quality of childcare reliably or validly.
5. Parents lie about their childcare, to themselves and to others.
6. Parental choice of childcare is motivated by concern for personal convenience, rather than by concern for the quality of care their children receive.
7. Parents choose childcare of lower quality because they make a trade-off, sacrificing quality for personal convenience and for flexibility in their work, family, and childcare arrangements (evidence to the contrary will be reported in Chapter 7).

Thus, a set of "factual" conclusions, though based on questionable evidence, faulty inference, and much circularity, came to be believed by many. An old attitude that disparaged parents came to shape an articulate, if not dominant social philosophy within the childcare profession.

Helburn's view of *America's Child Care Problem* may or may not represent the mainstream of the profession's philosophy. That is hard to tell, because it is expressed by an influential literature that has not received much rebuttal. Nevertheless, most childcare professionals are simply dedicated to their work, trying to improve the quality of care for children. More approval might be found for Joan Lombardi's *Time to Care: Redesigning Child Care to Promote Education, Support Families, and Build Communities* (2003). Former head of the U. S. Child Care Bureau, she seeks broad public support for quality childcare based on values such as caring, education, and equity. Although balanced by family-support services, her vision, nevertheless, is primarily to create a system of care and education services. Her tone about parents is positive, but parents are not the solution. This is basically a profession of "supply-siders" whose direct practice and primary concern is developing good childcare for children.

However, although Sally Sly's snobbery about selfish parents and scandalous daycare has become more sophisticated, the bias is persistently evident in the discomfort felt with the diverse childcare arrangements that families seek, in attitudes dismissive of parental choice, in obsession with quality rating scales, and in advocacy of a universal system of professional-quality childcare that would not have to depend upon parental choice.

The illuminating example of this attitude mentioned in the Preface bears repeating: "We already know what quality of care is. Why ask parents?!" This social philosophy is the Achilles' heel that jeopardizes the success of a worthy profession. It is a profession that cares about children, but still must learn to care about parents. This fatal flaw prevents the profession from engaging parents and families within the world in which they live. Perhaps the remedy is a close look at the natural ability with which parents make their decisions about childcare.

CHAPTER 3

PARENTS HAVE THEIR REASONS

"Common sense is wisdom dressed in working clothes."

~Ralph Waldo Emerson

T he flaw inherent in use of quality rating scales isn't just the negative bias about parental judgment, and it isn't just the invalidity of jumping the logical chasm between evaluation and description. Perhaps the most fundamental flaw is the lack of relevance. These measuring sticks ignore the diversity of resources within reach of individual families and for that reason are of questionable applicability. The highly abstract idea—*quality of childcare*—is worth considering, but, when childcare is measured against idealized standards and taken out of context of the situations parents face, the relevance is illusory.

It is not plausible to suppose that parents—any parents—can rely upon quality ratings in choosing childcare, or even heavily upon a set of "quality indicators" that are more empirically based, such as *group size*—caring for a manageable number of children. Parents must use a variety of practical criteria as well. They must make reasonable choices. People do not do what isn't feasible. It would be psychotic not to consider proximity or transportation—time and distance—for example. Every decision about childcare has an ecology—an environmental and social context—as well as purpose. Choices are not made in the realm of make-believe.

It would be make-believe also to suppose that parents do not use their own values in choosing childcare. In real life, the nature of parental choice of childcare involves a factual and evaluative appraisal of a complex mixture of values, circumstances, and opportunities close at hand. It is the complexity of real life that explains the diversity of the arrangements that parents make. The evidence presented in this chapter supports the following simple proposition— Proposition A. *Parental choices reflect a blend of values, circumstances, and opportunities.*

Parents have their reasons. To understand why parents make the choices that they do, and to appreciate how rational those choices are, it will help to examine some of the reasons that make sense to them. Here are twelve. The first four reasons are so basic that they define the feasibility of daily life. The next four reasons arise from the social support available within the family's immediate environment. And the last four reasons involve characteristics that parents believe will contribute directly to the quality of care the child will experience. All of these reasons involve a blend of practical and value-based considerations. For any chosen arrangement, the facts will vary—and the values too. Hence the wide diversity of arrangements.

1. Family composition: Parents play the hand they were dealt. The first principle is that parents play the hand they were dealt. They tend to use the family resources they have and turn to something else when they don't. Especially in low-income families, some two-earner families stagger shifts when they can, to avoid using childcare. When an older brother or sister is looking after a younger sibling, the foremost reason is because there is an older brother or sister. Parents who turn to care in the family home of an unrelated neighbor most likely do not have a relative living with them or near enough to be available for childcare. Single parents are much more likely than married couples to use paid childcare, even though they can hardly afford it, and single parents who live solo are twice as likely to use paid care as single parents who live in a household where there is another adult. Household composition really matters. It is a powerful reality. It provides the most obvious way of doing things, and all other choices are apt to be secondary considerations.

2. Proximity: Saving distance, time, effort, and energy. When parents go outside the home for childcare, proximity matters. The distances traveled for childcare tell an important story about convenience. Most people seek arrangements close to home, while a small minority find it close to work. As a simple statement, that is no surprise;

but the power of proximity is strong and systematic. You would have to keep doubling the distance of the radius around homes to encounter the same frequency of childcare arrangements.[6] Distance data illustrate what George Zipf (1949, 1965) referred to as the "principle of least effort" in human behavior. I have found this fundamental principle borne out dozens of times in employee surveys. Parents do not waste any more energy than they have to. Of course, the distances are shorter in compact, densely populated neighborhoods, as well as in communities in which information networks are lively enough to improve access to choices. Over the decades, travel distances got longer when the demand for childcare increased and the supply of available care shrank, as the supply of stay-at-home moms entered the workforce.

Proximity competes with other values. A center director may boast of how far parents are willing to travel to her program, and the fact that parents will do that is evidence that parents are willing to sacrifice some convenience for the quality of care they seek. But all things being equal, which they never quite are, people are as smart as they can be about proximity. Economy of time, motion, effort, and energy is almost instinctual, even though it may be trumped by other values. Working parents are not exempt from the laws of nature that we all need for survival. And parents aren't the only ones who benefit from their choice of proximity—there are the children in transit and the entire family, too, and maybe even the environment.

3. Finding childcare to fit work shifts, or vice versa. A dominant fact of life for employed parents is seeking job shifts to fit the times childcare is available, finding childcare to match their shifts, or staggering shifts so childcare is not needed. Since families differ, diversity on the demand side requires diversity in the supply of care. Who provides the childcare to fit with non-traditional work schedules? A sample of providers used by families receiving childcare assistance offers an answer (Emlen 1998b). Providers were asked what services they offered: care during evenings, on weekends, overnight, drop-in, and when children are sick. Among providers of all types of care, centers stood out for the paucity of non-traditional care offered. Childcare provided in family homes, whether in or out of the child's home and whether by grandmothers, relatives or non-relatives, carried the burden of the demanding days and hours of care. Centers do create a stable source of childcare, but kith and kin and neighbor-

---

[6] You can substitute travel time for distance and find similar results.

hood caregivers are the ones who bring diversity to the accessibility of care, so essential for many parents.

These sources of childcare diversity also play a role in the multiple arrangements that perhaps a third of employed parents use, some of it paid and some unpaid. Eminently practical for coverage of work schedules, they also are sought because a child may need varied experiences, such as an educational program in a large group part of the day and low-key situation with personal attention for the rest of the day. Multiple arrangements are sometimes disparaged as "make-shift," "crazy-quilt," or "major juggling," as if the ideal were full-day care in one place. It is true that many scramble to find childcare to meet challenging shifts or changing schedules that are sometimes thoughtlessly implemented by employers. But it makes no sense to blame the parents. The diversity of full-day, part-time, or multiple part-time arrangements is legitimate demand.

4. Known relationships: Familiarity and trust. Parents reach out to someone they already know and trust to look after their children. They want a known person they have experiential evidence to trust, or else someone they know about and have been put in touch with through someone they trust. They seek continuity with the familiar and are slow to expose themselves or their child to a strange situation.

A trusted caregiver may have faults that others would be unwilling to excuse, and different parents have different standards in assessing health or safety—different levels of tolerance for hazards or harms they see or learn about. Yet knowing those relationships personally as part of a network of known relationships is how parents are able to make and confirm their judgments. But parents want to be able to answer the question: "Is my child safe and secure?"

Still more important to parents may be observing a warmth of feeling for their child. That may be easier for parents to observe in the care provided by relatives and other unregulated family-home caregivers, than in centers, and account for many choices.

5. Neighborhood and supportive social networks. Families are embedded in neighborhoods. The importance of neighborhood is related to proximity and to known relationships, with an added cultural dimension. Parents choose informal childcare in part because it *is* embedded in supportive social networks rooted in the neighborhood. Whether childcare is in the child's own home, in another home, or in a center, the neighborhood ecology of childcare is critical. Does the child feel safe and secure? That partly depends on the safety of the neighborhood. Is it hazardous, sterile, or rich in natural supportive relationships? Here too, the quality of the childcare hinges on this immediate environment.

The health of neighborhoods seems to get attention in public policy only in scattered spurts, but one group has shown an impressive ability to link it to the quality of childcare. Tony Earls and his wife, Maya Carlson, and their Harvard research team have been conducting a long-term study of child development in the context of some 300 Chicago neighborhoods (Sampson 1997). They looked at formal characteristics of community-based organizations and also at informal characteristics within neighborhoods, such as trust, reciprocity, and shared values regarding the raising of children. They call these combined characteristics "collective efficacy." As a determinant of either social disorder or quality of life for children, they found this indicator even more powerful than wealth and poverty, race and ethnic composition, immigrant concentration, and residential stability.

6. The price of childcare—and its value. Providers of family care charge less than centers that meet a payroll, and parents using care provided by kith and kin are of course attracted by the lower cost. In centers, the labor costs of high quality of care make it more expensive. But how do parents put a price on the warmth and interest in the child that lies at the heart of quality? And how do the caregivers put a price on their services? Especially in informal settings, warmth and interest in a child is not so costly. Motivations are complex, and there is more to economic behavior than economics.

Even paid childcare is infused with service motives. In part it is an altruistic response to the needs of others, Market–rate studies (Emlen 1995b) show that family daycare providers often discount the prices they charge parents in response to family needs, including "two-fers" when there's a second child. They use sliding scales with a frequency that makes these already low-paid service providers look like an army of United Way supporters.

Informally arranged care by grandmothers and other relatives, friends, neighbors, and other unrelated persons, is one of the great examples of direct, interpersonal helping in our nation's history. There is an exchange of services for some form of compensation, but for the paid caregiver, the motivation also includes rewards other than money. In a study of caregivers for family, friends, and neighbors in the state of Washington (Brandon 2002), only 4 percent cited "need the income" as the main reason for providing care, while 57 percent said it was helping out a friend or relative, 12 percent said it was helping the child or children, and 24 percent said it was because they enjoyed being with the child or children.

The price of center care may reflect quality due to the cost of staffing, but much of the quality in the care provided by kith and kin is not reflected in the price. From a parent's point of view, informally arranged care is a valued choice and a legitimate part of the childcare market.

7. Caregivers who share their values. There is diversity in the values parents seek as they choose childcare. Some look for a caregiver who seems similar and seems to share the same values. Similarities in race and ethnicity, common national origin, or other cultural commonalities may provide assured respect, and cultural continuity for the children, and the values sought. Having access to a caregiver "who shares my values" can be a challenge in the childcare marketplace and a strong reason for turning to family, relatives, friends, and neighbors.

8. Caregivers who bring experience that's new and different. Parents also look for caregivers who bring something new and different. This is from a chapter I wrote with Pacific Oaks researcher Elizabeth Prescott:

> Parents may look for a home that complements, in some way, the experiences that they themselves can provide. For example, a single mother may want a home where the provider's husband enjoys and interacts with the children, a parent may want a child to have the experience of being the oldest or youngest among children, or a young parent may want a grandmotherly person or caregiver from the same cultural background. These may be very different criteria from those viewed as important by the professional community, and we are not ready to dismiss the wisdom of parent choices. (Emlen 1992)

Whether kith or kin or family daycare, the caregivers whom parents find are not professional experts. They respond to the needs of children by doing something they more or less know how to do from experience in raising their own children. It falls within the realm of ordinary behavior.

Of course, experience doesn't necessarily mean high quality. A recent study (Kontos 1995) found that training, not experience, predicted quality of care. While that may be true, the importance of experience has not been richly explored. Several authors have given some attention to how parents and caregivers are different (Peters 1992), and some differences in experience are worth noting. Many caregivers are older than the parents they help and have raised more children—their own and others. Some are grandmothers whom parents turn to also for recipes and advice. A wealth of child-rearing and childcare experience is one of the many ways that the capacities and motivations of informal caregivers complement those of the employed parents who engage them. These differences make possible the massive division of labor that occurs in society between informal caregivers and the employed parents who depend on them.

9. Home and neighborhood as a learning environment. One piece of flotsam on the waves of advocacy has been the classification of care as either "custodial" or "developmental." The term "developmental" was often equated with "educational," and this implied that professionally trained childcare providers were needed in order for children to learn. The term "custodial" meant "mere custody" as in the warehousing children in centers, but they also used the term to apply to refer to unregulated, informal family care as a category. It was an unfortunate tainting of the core values of care giving. The classification disregarded the truths discovered by parents every day and catalogued by Elizabeth Prescott (1972) in her pioneering research. She discovered and documented how care in family homes affords a rich, "fuzzy-warm" child-rearing environment with myriad learning opportunities in individual play and in simple social interaction, along with natural observational experiences in the kitchen or from a visit by the plumber or other neighborhood figure.

Descriptive categories are easily given invidious or virtuous connotations. One illustration can be found in an inference that Suzanne Helburn and Barbara Bergmann make from an interesting study of family childcare in a Northeast working-class urban community (Zinsser 1991). Helburn and Bergmann featured a selective portrait of family childcare by saying:

> Zinsser's caregivers said that they communicated very little with the parents about the children, evidently because both parents and caregiver saw the arrangement as purely custodial. (2002, p. 102)

The observations are interesting, but the inference following the words "evidently because" reveals the bias. The comment also seems to imply the desirability of childcare reforms that would try to change the values and behavior of an entire social class.

10. Individuation: the parent's ultimate test. "Is this just what my child needs?" Parents judge quality by whether it works for their own children. Does *my* child feel safe and secure? Does *my* child get enough individual attention? Does the caregiver like *my* child? Their assessment is individualized, not general. What good is some general seal of approval for the quality of care of a facility if the caregiver doesn't like or respond well to *your* child? In choosing childcare, parents ask whether the care meets their own child's needs.

And in doing so, parents don't just consider what is happening within a childcare setting, but also within their family. They judge childcare by its contribution to the child's quality of life. Children differ in age and gender, of course, and the composition of ages within a family also differs. There is a tendency sometimes to think of childcare as happening to one child at a time, but parents work out solutions for all their children in ways that interact. Individualizing a child's needs is complex.

Another way that children differ is in health—both emotional health and physical condition. Perhaps 1 in 10 may have a disability, emotional and behavioral problem, or a "special need." In being individually different these children are really just like all children, only more so. Their special needs pose a challenge for parents, of course, and they challenge caregivers or childcare facilities to be inclusive (Brennan 2003). The parents of these children are looking for some extra level of effort, sensitivity, knowledge, and simple willingness to respond to their child as an individual. Just like all parents.

11. Group size: Caregivers who take fewer children. Way back in the late 60s and early 70s when I was studying family daycare arrangements that were privately and informally made, unlicensed, unregistered and unregulated, I noticed a striking phenomenon. Like the Song Sparrow that keeps to a clutch size of six, even when accommodating the egg of a Cowbird, providers of care in family homes tended to limit "group size" to what they can manage. They kept the numbers of children in care well below any licensing limit or regulatory standard there might have been. As their own families grew older they were filling a half-empty nest. Like the song sparrow, altogether they seldom exceeded six, including their own. They didn't need a licensing law to curb their numbers.

What are group sizes like today? Over the years, great strides have been made in licensing or at least officially registering family childcare homes and in encouraging professional training of those providers. These trends occurred at the same time that increased labor force participation of mothers brought increased demand to the doors of a proportionately smaller population of stay-at-home mothers. The result has been larger group sizes within the regulated sector of family care. It is also possible that referral services and other professional encouragement to use the existing supply of regulated care also contributes to the trend toward larger group sizes.

Oregon conducts a statewide household survey every two years, and one of the questions asked is if anybody in the household is providing childcare for pay (Partnership 1995; 2000). The results have shown a significant increase in the number of children in the care that is regulated, although there are still many unregulated providers who only take one, two, or three children.

In the year 2000, of those childcare providers giving care in their homes (not in the child's home) and doing it for pay, 15 percent cared only for children they were related to. Of those caring for non-relatives only, 40 percent were not doing it regularly and mostly for only one or two children. Among providers who were caring for unrelated children regularly and for pay, the average number of children cared for was 3.6 and the group size reported for a typical day was 3.5.

However, the averages don't tell the story. Although 63 percent of the regular providers were only caring for one, two, or three children, that accounted for only one-third of the children. Two-thirds of the children were in groups of at least four—more precisely: 15 percent in homes with four or five children, 28 percent in groups of six or seven, and 24 percent in groups of eight to twelve. By historical standards, those are big groups for childcare in family homes, and the trend toward larger groups is likely to continue.

It is worth pausing to appreciate the significance of group size. A group of six already involves twice as many children as most parents have experience relating to, and is five times as complex as a group of three. The social dynamics of a group of children becomes dramatically more complex as the size of the group increases. In a group of three there are only three individual child-to-child relationships occurring, but in a group of six there are 15, and in a group of 10 children there are 45 little relationships possible. The equation for the number of relationships is N-squared minus N, divided by 2. The significance is that the bigger the group, the more is required in adult control, direction, leadership, creativity, training, experience, and staffing.

Has provider training kept pace with the increase in the size of the group? Or are many parents right to be hesitant about choosing the bigger homes despite the increased proportion of providers who have become professionally trained? A well-regarded study (Kontos et al 1995) found that the larger regulated homes provide a higher quality of care than do unregulated providers. That may be true, but it may be wise to doubt how representative a research sample can ever be of an unlisted population of informal care arrangements. And it may be wise to suspect a possible circularity between the findings and the measurement, when the operational definition of quality is the frequency of social interactions with the teacher or caregiver, which of course would be more characteristic of larger groups.

12. Flexibility. A final issue that parents consider concerns the source of their flexibility. Flexibility is a remarkable human ability to make choices that are both feasible and desirable—desirable in terms of their values and feasible in terms of the constraints and opportunities present in the parent's immediate environment. The constraints may be commanding and make sense to parents, and the enabling resources that parents use are precious.

CHAPTER 4

THE SOURCES OF FLEXIBILITY

"To me, the defining trait of working mothers is flexibility."

~Judson Culbreth, editor in chief, *Working Mother* magazine

When parents make decisions about childcare there are a host of practical considerations that make their choices feasible. These practicalities are often characterized as providing geographic proximity, convenience, affordability, availability, and accessibility. They provide parents with the flexibility they need to arrive at a feasible decision. Most decisively, parents gain or lose flexibility from the latitude allowed by job and work schedules, from how responsibilities within the family are divided or shared, and from how demanding or accommodating a childcare provider can be. They draw the resources for their flexibility from many sources.

Our research findings suggest that flexibility is the nexus and net value of all of the family's resources that parents can draw upon to manage work, family life, and childcare. Their adaptive and creative ability to do that is a form of human intelligence that can be defined and measured in terms of the resources parents use for flexibility. In evidence presented in the next chapters, flexibility is found to be of central importance in understanding the dynamics of choice and its outcomes.

First, however, some discourse on the *concept of flexibility*, with background on how this idea was made applicable to issues concerning family, work, and childcare, as parents making their decisions about childcare. This chapter expands the concept of flexibility by identifying its sources, as offered in Proposition B: *Flexibility is the ability to solve a puzzle of many pieces that come mainly from the parent's immediate environment of work, family, and childcare; or, as in the case of financial flexibility, are mediated through those three main sources.*

Flexibility solves the puzzle. When parents strive to combine child rearing, family life, working, and use of non-parental childcare, they balance priorities, juggle schedules, and make choices to fit their values and circumstances. As we shall see, parents are likely to make the best childcare choices possible, given the resources at their disposal. For this they need flexibility. They have a giant puzzle to solve. It is never a standardized puzzle on a card table with a fixed number of cut pieces. Each family has a different puzzle to solve, its configuration shaped by resources and events. Furthermore, it is a fluid puzzle, always in motion, with pieces that may change shape suddenly. As chief puzzle-solvers, parents rely on the resources available and on their own creative ability to shape and reshape the pieces and fit them together.

The key to solving this puzzle is the flexibility: The pursuit of any purpose requires either an anatomical capacity to stretch or bend without breaking or a behavioral capacity to adapt and to fashion alternative strategies that work. In general, that is the core meaning of flexibility. Without it all complex purposeful activity is frozen. Flexibility is a capacity at the core of how things get done. It involves puzzle-solving as a creative ability, but it requires having resources at hand to make alternative strategies possible.

Flexibility is a resource more precious than gold. Nobody knows quite how much it is worth, but everybody wants it. It is in limited supply, and all the institutions of society compete for it. Parents and families are a primary source of it, but not the only ones. Inventive as they may be, parents can't make it out of thin air. It has to come from somewhere. All the practicalities of living—the demands and necessities, the feasibilities and resources—melt down to possession of flexibility. It is the universal currency that makes the business of living possible. Malleable and exchangeable, flexibility can take many forms. Out of this element, parents invent unique personal solutions that allow them to prevail in a challenging world.

Behind the metaphors of puzzles and gold, lie some questions to answer: Why is flexibility a fundamental necessity? Where does it come from? Who is competing for it and in what ways? Is flexibility an adaptive and creative form of intelligence or an environmental resource, or is it both? How can the dimensions of flexibility be measured?

To capture both the simplicity of the basic idea and the complexity of the varied contributions that make it possible, it helps to define flexibility in terms of those resources in a parent's environment that allow them—for valued purposes—to reach an adaptive and creative solution.

Flexibility is not a luxury, however. It involves the management of time and distance. Flexibility is as fundamental and objective as time and space. We all shape our lives within the physical constraints of time and distance. How parents combine work, family life, and childcare is a hundred lessons in geography and the management of time. A parent's need for proximity, time, and convenience is not a luxury. It is as basic as conserving energy, which for all animals is a key to survival. Flexibility is what gives parents effective and efficient means to prevail while responding to the pressures of time and the demands of geography.

The flexibility that working parents possess in their lives has compelling immediacy for them in meeting the demands of work and family. They must have it. There is an ultimate physical limit to the number of hours in a day. Time, which comes packaged in hours per day and days per week or month, is a finite resource, even for the efficient, talented, and ingenious. There is no escape, even for the sleep-deprived. Time is a physical dimension of daily life that allows or constrains all activity. So if on a regular basis your life is tightly packed with long hours on the job, frequent overtime and new deadlines, getting from one place to another, child rearing, childcare arrangements, elder care, cooking, eating, and the other activities that make up a day, then you have little time for accidents or emergencies or special events, for flat tires or traffic jams or old cars that won't start, for soccer games or teacher conferences or scrapes with the police, for illness or family crises, for births or deaths, or for friends, or for a quiet walk in the woods. Emergencies, surprise events, and unplanned extras are inevitable. They too are part of life. Things happen. You need some flexibility to deal with them. In the management of childcare, work, and family life, flexibility is a fundamental need.

Where does flexibility come from? For employed parents, flexibility mostly comes from their work schedules, from shared responsibility within the family, or from accommodating caregivers. There are other sources of flexibility for parents, such as finances and transportation; but work, family, and childcare are the big three, I have found, and they are implicated in other sources as well. For example, financial flexibility may relate to family flexibility or childcare flexibility in complex ways. Two parents have more flexibility than single parents and if they have two incomes they may either reduce or enhance their family flexibility and put their financial flexibility at risk. Another example is transportation. Rosalind Barnett has linked job flexibility, commuting time, and after-school care to parental concerns about it (2006). The importance of the geography of convenience is highlighted also by the notable differences in the proximity of childcare between urban, suburban, and rural settings. In general, however, the ecology of daycare plays out substantially in the amount of work, family, and caregiver flexibility that a parent has.

My definition of flexibility expands on ordinary usage by incorporating its multiple sources, including of course the flexibility that comes from work arrangements and related employer policies. By now "flextime" is a familiar idea, as employers modify work schedules and shifts, and create other ways to facilitate where, when, and how work gets done. Implemented in pursuit of productivity and to accommodate employee demand, the business case for job flexibility has been studied for some years and is well recognized. Because flexible work arrangements are so important, they have received the bulk of attention in work and family policy and research. See, for example, the literature of the Families and Work Institute, the Sloan Work and Family Research Network at Boston College, or WorldatWork. As a result, flexibility has usually been synonymous with workplace flexibility.

Work flexibility is certainly a huge piece of the puzzle; but there are other pieces too, coming from other sources in a parent's life. How does childcare fit into the picture, for example? And family? Defining flexibility in terms of the whole puzzle is more likely to provide answers about outcomes. It appears that parents compensate for a shortage of flexibility in one area of life by finding an abundance of it in another, if they can. Flexibility has to come from somewhere—if not from one source, then another. The research will show that a parent's success lies in the net amount of flexibility they can acquire from any or all sources.

Broadening the scope of the concept of flexibility in this way, to include multiple sources—family and childcare as well as work— bears some connection to the concept of *balancing* work, family, and the rest of life, which has been discussed by many investigators (Drago 2007; Galinsky 1999: 2000) for example. I see *flexibility* and *balancing* are kindred concepts. In the findings that will be reported below in support of Proposition E, what I call a *flexibility solution* is, in effect, a balancing strategy, in which parents compensate for a dearth of flexibility of one kind by seeking a more feasible source of flexibility. Both are neutral about the strategies sought, since that is up to the parents. Flexibility is a more microscopic way of analyzing the balancing process, while the term *balancing* seems descriptively to connote a more deliberate purpose. I suspect that, imagining a study of employees, the scores measuring total amount of flexibility from three sources, as shown later in Table 7.2, would correlate strongly with scores measuring work, family, and life balance, which I did not try to measure.

In thinking about flexibility and its sources, there is another ambiguity to deal with. Although parents deploy whatever flexibility their environment provides, they are the puzzle-solvers; so in that sense, they themselves are a source. It is understandable that parents are exhorted to "be flexible." The editor in chief of *Working Mother* magazine, Judson Culbreth, stated in a 1997 issue, "To me, the defining trait of working mothers is flexibility." The feature article in that issue was about "The Improv Mom"—lauding working mothers for "being flexible" through improvising. However, the article's author, Susan Seliger, also gave credit to Improv Moms for having sparked changes in the workplace by "urging companies to become as flexible and innovative as they themselves have learned to be. And we're seeing the fruits of their efforts in more flextime, better maternity and paternity leave and child care policies" (1997). The author was right in recognizing the individual's creative contribution to flexibility, and she was right also in urging companies to become an objective source of flexibility, thus recognizing implicitly that flexibility is not simply a matter of willingness, motivation, and talent, or just a skill to be learned. Flexibility is also a resource to be drawn from the parent's immediate environment.

Who competes for flexibility, and in what ways? Flexibility is universally precious, and not just for parents. Although families and organizations may share purposes in common, they both seek to operate at their own convenience. Everyone competes for flexibility, and for every person or organization it has to come from somewhere. When businesses, schools, or other organizations seek flexibility for their operations and productivity, where does that flexibility come from? Some may come from increasing internal efficiency and some of it comes from externalizing the sources and cost of flexibility by relying on the family and childcare flexibility of their employees.

Companies are discovering "just in time" ways to manage their own resources, but they also draw on an employee's supply of flexibility when they assign fixed work schedules, rotating shifts, overtime versus "comp" time, longer work weeks, quotas for billable hours, severe absenteeism policies, and when they schedule business meetings early, late, or at the lunch hour. Such practices led the sociologist Lewis Coser (1974) to write about "greedy institutions" that make omnivorous demands and diminish the opportunities for competing claims.

Coser's description presented an extreme form of a universal tension. All organizations, to some degree, seek to operate for their own convenience, demanding flexibility from others. Schools, services, companies, families, and childcare providers all focus on the flexibility they need. For example, within the family, divisions of labor and shared responsibilities are ways of allocating or even creating flexibility. Childcare providers often are no exception, sometimes requiring some of a parent's supply of flexibility in order to run a high-quality program. Flexibility, in general, is a highly prized resource. All of these institutions share some goals and have some common interests, but the mutual interests are not always recognized and the reciprocities not always negotiated.

Do employers compete for all the flexibility that employed parents can produce, not allowing the parents the flexibility they need in order to manage well? Is this a tug of war? Or can there be a balance that works for both? Those are policy questions addressed in Chapter 9.

Family flexibility, work flexibility, and childcare flexibility: Surprising lessons from absenteeism. My own discovery that families and employers were competing for flexibility came during the 1980s from conducting a large number of employee surveys for many different employers, examining how employees managed childcare and elder care, and its impact on the workplace. Surprising lessons about work flexibility and family flexibility emerged from analysis of differences in employee absenteeism that reflected differences in the source of flexibility relied upon—work environment, family solutions, or childcare. The surveys were of the entire workforce— men, women, with or without children.

The history of research on employee absenteeism reveals how slow investigators were to recognize the flexibility issue in absenteeism. More than 60 years ago, at the height of World War II, when women were called to the work force for a workweek of six 8-hour days, a study of absenteeism was conducted at a war plant in Elgin, Illinois (Schenet 1945). The study found that women had three times more absenteeism than the men, but the researchers couldn't explain why. Back then, and for nearly four decades afterward, researchers measured one variable after another, from attendance norms, job satisfaction, occupation, and size of organization or work unit to health and even menstrual cycles, without focusing on the ordinary everyday behaviors related to childcare responsibilities and types of arrangements. They came close, studying the effects of age, sex, family size, and travel distance of work; but based on two comprehensive reviews, in 95 studies (Murchinsky 1977) and one to 431 studies (Porwoll 1980), none of the researchers had made the connection to childcare.

Actually, two studies warrant mentioning. In a 1962 study of a large Parisian workforce (Isambert-Jamati 1962), French researchers did report higher absenteeism rates for women with family obligations. However, they drew no general conclusions from this other than about sex and social position, even though they found women with dependent children who co-coordinated schedules with husbands or arranged to stand in for each other so as to prevent management from discovering their absence. Then, in a 1980 study, Paula Englander-Golden and Glenn Barton concluded that "child care rather than personal illness appears to be the major variable which mediates sex differences in absence from work." Neither of these studies, however, linked employee absenteeism, by gender, to types of childcare, and kinds of jobs.

An opportunity to examine those relationships came in 1983, with a research grant from U.S. Department of Health and Human Services, when my colleagues and I in Portland, Oregon, responded to interest expressed by area employers in having an objective assessment of the childcare needs of employees, sorting the hype from the evidence. A printed report to employers called "Hard to Find and Difficult to Manage: The Effects of Child Care on the Workplace" (Emlen 1984) presented the findings of a survey of 8,121 employees at 33 companies and agencies.

The study recast absenteeism, which had been seen only as an employee behavior problem, a "women's problem," or as a childcare problem. But the landscape came into view when comparing male and female employees, with and without children, as well as the kinds of arrangements made for the children (in three crucial categories: care by spouse or other adult at home, any kind of out-of-home daycare, and care by child—usually an older brother or sister.

Unsurprisingly, absenteeism rates were higher for employees with children, for mothers, and for childcare out of home or by siblings. Fathers with a spouse at home had low absenteeism rates equal to those of men who had no children at all. The highest absenteeism rates came from women whose children were in out-of-home care or who were relying on care by a child. The detailed picture of absenteeism that those mothers reported, compared to fathers with a spouse at home, was:

> 65 percent higher in days missed (an estimated 5.1 days per year difference), 278 percent higher in times late (a difference of 13.6 times per year), 74 percent higher in leaving work early (a difference of 5.8 times per year), and 210 percent higher in interruptions (a difference of 53.1 times per year)....A noteworthy variation was that fathers missed as many days per year as mothers when the arrangement was care-by-child (13.4 days per year for fathers; 13.0 for mothers). (Emlen 1984)

Although different arrangements for children accounted for sizable differences in absenteeism, in the bigger picture, when taking the family's division of labor into account, absenteeism was revealed not to be a "women's problem" but a family solution. Absenteeism for men was low for the same reason that the women's rate was high. It reflected who was carrying the childcare responsibilities that made it possible for the employee to be at work—and, more than half the time, for a spouse to be at work as well.

Understanding absenteeism takes a workforce perspective, and the kind of job is part of the picture. For a balanced view of sources of absenteeism, here's a calculation based on the Portland study *Hard to Find* as quoted by Dana Friedman of The Conference Board in *Linking Work-Family Issues to the Bottom Line* (1991):

> If the workforce misses about nine days per year, men who have no children miss 7.5 days. Add a half

a day for being a father, one day for using out-of-home care or 5.5 days if the children look after themselves. This brings the total for men to 13.5 days. Women without children start at 9.5 days absent. Two days can be added if kids are in care outside the home or 3.5 days if she is a single parent. If she is in management, she will miss a day or two less, but she will be late to work more often since her job will allow it. Having a family income of $30,000 or more saves women in management and professional positions nearly two days or a half-day for women who are not in that position. The income difference saves men one day at either occupational level. Take off several days if the company's personnel policies severely clamp down on absenteeism, but add stress.

Understanding absenteeism not just as a problem of time loss but also as a family solution may seem counterintuitive, but the idea that absenteeism has a positive side becomes easier to grasp when you realize how much absenteeism varies with different jobs and how much it is part of the flexibility that employees need to get the work done. The study identified absenteeism itself as an informal source of flexibility for employed parents and for families. There are two faces of absenteeism. On the one hand, it results from a lack of family flexibility; on the other hand, it is an unofficial, tolerated, informal source of work flexibility. Wide variation in absenteeism is found associated with different job requirements, occupations, and levels of responsibility within companies (Emlen and Koren 1984, 11).[7] Some jobs allow absence more easily than others. This is especially true with coming late, leaving early, and for interruptions during the workday, which are apt to go unrecorded, perhaps unnoticed, and the time loss made up for in subsequent productivity. Time missed for family or personal emergencies provides latitude and a safety valve. In our later study, we discovered that flexible work

---

[7] Similar ground was covered with other Portland State colleagues in predicting absenteeism when considering employee responsibilities for care of children, elders, or adults with disability: Neal, Margaret, Nancy Chapman, Berit Ingersoll-Dayton, and Arthur Emlen, 1993, *Balancing Work and Caregiving for Children, Adults, and Elders*. Newbury Park, CA: Sage Publications.

schedules, personnel policies, and management practices for dealing with childcare problems in a department did not predict the number of days missed but did predict the incidence of the lesser forms of time loss (Neal et al 1993, 84). In that study, we found three resources consistently related to lower stress for employed parents: work-schedule flexibility, ease of finding and maintaining childcare, and satisfaction with childcare arrangements (85).

For many employees, some degree of work flexibility is so essential to the feasibility of working that a draconian policy of zero tolerance for absenteeism would be virtually impossible to sustain. It would produce high levels of stress and would likely lead to a more costly turnover in personnel. Many employees, including employed parents, are able to manage jobs that realistically cannot tolerate much time loss, but to make that possible, these employees have other sources of flexibility in their lives. In two-parent families, they may stagger shifts in order to cover both work schedules without using childcare; and in single–parent families, a lack of resources for flexibility within the household is a major predictor of the use of paid childcare. An analysis of data from the Oregon Population Survey (Partnership 1995 and 2000, Table 6) found that single parents who live solo were twice as likely to use paid childcare as single parents who shared housing with another adult: 68 percent vs. 36 percent in 1995, and 55 percent vs. 27 percent in 2000.

Caregiver flexibility. The third major possible source of flexibility, in addition to work and family, is a non-parental childcare provider, a caregiver who can meet the parent's work schedule. For many parents, the search for a flexible caregiver is critical. A consumer study by Oregon's Adult and Family Services illustrates how important the fit between work schedule and access to childcare is for families receiving public assistance. For 41 percent of the parents in the consumer survey, their work or training required childcare on evenings or weekends. According to the Bureau of Labor Statistics, this was more than twice the 17 percent national average for nontraditional shift work (1997). In the Oregon survey, 25 percent said their work shift rotated, so their childcare had to vary also. For 35 percent of all surveyed parents, the schedule changed—either daily, weekly, or monthly. And 60 percent of parents had no other adult living in the household with whom they could share childcare responsibilities. So, having neither family flexibility nor work flexibility, where do these parents find the flexibility they need? They must find and rely upon an accommodating caregiver. The consumers surveyed perceived family daycare and especially care by relatives as providing more accessibility and flexibility of services than centers. This perception was validated by other survey reports of services provided: evenings, weekends, overnight, for drop-in, or when children are sick. In the childcare market, dramatic differences in the flexibility provided by caregivers are shown in Table 2.1—differences that influence the choice of care.

Table 2.1. Percent Offering Non-Traditional Care, by Type of Provider

Care Provided	Center	Family Day-care	Home of Relative	Child's Home by Live-in Relative	Child's Home by Comes-in Relative	Child's Home by Comes-in Non-relative	Child's Home by Live-in Non-relative
Evenings	10	53	69	72	68	80	71
Weekends	6	46	66	68	65	68	63
Overnight	3	35	42	42	37	42	34
Drop-in	35	56	40	19	30	43	12
Child sick	3	40	63	58	71	63	59
N	266	1136	635	105	116	139	41

N=2438 childcare providers reimbursed by Adult and Family Services, Oregon Department of Human Resources, childcare assistance program, 1998.

A sharp example of caregiver flexibility was reported by AFL-CIO flight attendants who were flying one of three national or regional airlines (Desrosiers 1997)—a sub-sample in the quality-of-care study. Considering the vagaries of air travel, a flight attendant who is also a mother would not have been in the sample without having an unusually flexible caregiver. Their scores on caregiver flexibility were at the top of the scale, which brings us to the issue of measurement.

CHAPTER 5

MEASURING QUALITY OF CARE
AND FLEXIBILITY

"If the result is contrary to the hypothesis, then you've
made a discovery."

~Enrico Fermi

I f the prevailing belief is that parents sacrifice quality for personal convenience—the profession's Achilles' heel—then
flexibility's positive relationship to quality of care is a discovery.
But first we need the data and the measurement and the findings.
This chapter provides evidence supporting two propositions—
Proposition C: *Parents have the ability to assess the quality of childcare and to
discriminate between quality and flexibility*; and Proposition D: *The overall
findings from multivariate analysis confirm that the three kinds of flexibility
parents report, taken together, are positively related to the quality of childcare they
report.*

Before reporting the findings, however, some introduction is required describing the purpose of the study, the sample, the methods
used, and the measures employed. The study was supported by the
United States Child Care Bureau (Emlen 1999b, 2000). The research
had two purposes. The primary purpose was to develop reliable
scales measuring quality of childcare, from a parent's point of view—
using parent data expressed in a parent's voice. The second purpose
was to examine which social conditions were associated with the
quality of care reported by parents—such as household income,
access to childcare, and the amount of flexibility contributed by work
arrangements, family life, and childcare resources. The validity of the

measures—especially of *quality* and *flexibility*— is important to examine, as well as characteristics of the sample.

Sample. By the end of July 1996, the original survey had produced a composite sample of 862 parent questionnaires from more than a dozen sources inclusive of a wide range of incomes, types of jobs, and types of childcare. The largest sub-sample was 264 US Bank employees who had children under age 13. Two other corporate samples were Boeing Aircraft employees using referral and counseling services and Mentor Graphics parents using an on-site child development center outstanding in quality. Members of the Association of Flight Attendants, AFL-CIO, who were living in Oregon and flying for three major airlines, provided a sample of parents with demanding work schedules, as compared to regular shifts. In addition to parents who found childcare informally on their own, the study included a sample of parents who had turned to resource and referral agencies for help in finding care. Among low-income parents, samples included families receiving public childcare assistance and those who did not. All levels of household income were represented—31% with less than $20,000, and 20% with $75,000 or more. The amount families spent monthly on childcare for all children, as a percentage of household income, provided a measure of affordability: the median spent was 9%, the middle half spent between 5% and 16%, with 29% spent by those least able to afford it.

An effort was made to find samples of parents of children with a disability, whose special childcare needs might present greater difficulty for parents and caregivers. As a result, 8 percent of the sample reported having a child with an emotional or behavioral problem requiring special attention. Though the overall sample consisted of current, active arrangements, many parents were facing a variety of challenges that contributed to a range in reported levels of quality of care. Two samples were selected for their recognized high quality, and, at the other extreme, were parents who had lodged complaints about care they were using.

Parents were asked about the main arrangement of their youngest child; so, in ages of the children, 69% of the sample children were under the age of 5, with a median age of 3. Among types of childcare, 89% of the parents were using paid care—38% in family daycare, 35% in centers, and 8% with a grandparent. The sample also included care in the child's home by caregivers who were unrelated. The children were in care a median of 30 hours per week, the middle half in care between 19 and 40 hours. The middle 50% of arrangements had already lasted from 5 to 24 months—the middle 80% from 2 to 36 months.

The sample came largely from Oregon—746 (87%), 58 from Washington, 44 from California, and 14 from 8 other states. The composite sample of 862 was dispersed across 253 zip-code areas.

An independent sample offered an opportunity to discover if the original scales could be replicated. Kyle Matchell and the Metropolitan Council on Child Care, in Kansas City, carried out a second survey in July 1997, and provided the investigators with the coded data to analyze. All parents in this sample (N=240) found their childcare through a community-based referral service—nearly three times as many in family homes as in centers, and 75 percent of the children were under 3 years of age (Emlen et al., 2000, p. 48). The Kansas City scales were strikingly similar to the original scales, and were equally, or more, reliable (p. 41).

Measuring quality of care, from a parent's perspective. In a survey including diverse samples, parents were asked about the current childcare arrangement of their youngest child, as they experienced it within the last four weeks. The written questionnaire posed simple statements such as *My child feels safe and secure, My caregiver is happy to see my child, My child gets a lot of individual attention, There are too many children being cared for at one time. The children watch too much TV*. Parents were asked whether that happened never, rarely, sometimes, often, or always— originally the scaling was without "rarely."

Parents may or may not have considered such questions before, but they found them easy to answer. For these questions, parents were not asked to make an abstract rating of quality or to report their satisfaction. They were asked to report the frequency with which they noticed recent events, specific situations, or characteristics of relationships. The largely descriptive statements drew upon observation as well as on their evaluative judgment. Although the word "quality' was not used, each statement did contain an implied evaluative assessment of what they had experienced. Based on a factor analysis of parent responses to 55 such items, those item responses that were most highly correlated, and had a similar underlying meaning, were grouped together to create several internally consistent scales that distinguished aspects of childcare quality, from a parent's point of view. Parents had succeeded in making reliable, discriminating judgments about their childcare.

The parent scales filled a gap in the literature, have been used by a number of other investigators, and have been included in a national compendium of measures of childcare quality, prepared by Child Trends, Inc. (Halle 2007). The compendium provides a review of existing measures and an appendix with the measures included. The review includes a concise presentation of the validity and applicability of the scales for use in parent surveys, when one does not know in advance which type of childcare the parent is using—center, family daycare, in-home care, or grandmother.

One of the scales, a composite 15-item scale, is used in the analysis reported later. See Table 5.1. Items such as *My child feels safe and secure* can be answered for a child of any age, in any type of childcare; but would statistical evidence confirm that the measurement scale have wide applicability without bias? In box-plot analyses, the level and variation of reported quality did not differ significantly for infants, toddlers, or preschoolers through age 6. Reported quality faded somewhat for school children, but the overall correlation was fairly low: r=.24. Statistical independence also assured unbiased applicability of the scale for use with different levels of household income and with the types of childcare—centers, family daycare, paid relative care, or paid in-home care by unrelated persons. Similar averages and variation in quality were found in all types of care and at every level of household income—under $5,000, $5,000-9,999, $10,000-14,999, $15,000-19,999, $20,000-29,999, $30,000-44,999, $45,000-64,999, $65,000-99,999, and $100,000 and above (Emlen, 1998; 1999).

Measuring flexibility. Flexibility is a familiar concept for working parents, often applied to "flextime" on the job—flexible work arrangements. But this paper advances a more fundamental concept of flexibility, as discussed earlier. It is both an assembly of resources and a creative problem-solving ability. For making childcare decisions, flexibility comes from multiple sources, including work, supportive family relationships, and accommodating childcare providers.

Flexibility, in general, is a resource so valuable that all people and organizations compete for it, including employers, because it is essential—indispensable—for successful pursuit of all purposeful activity. For employed parents it allows dealing with threatening emergencies or coping on a daily basis with the constraints of time and distance. A parent's behavioral flexibility is adaptive and creative. It requires gleaning, forging, crafting, and using whatever resources for flexibility can be developed from within that parent's immediate environment.

Table 5.1. 15-Item Parent Scale Measuring Quality of Childcare, N=862

Cronbach's Alpha Coefficient = .91

My child feels safe and secure in care.

The caregiver is warm and affectionate toward my child.

It's a healthy place for my child.

My child is treated with respect.

My child is safe with this caregiver.

My child gets a lot of individual attention.

My caregiver and I share information.

My caregiver is open to new information and learning.

My caregiver shows she (he) knows a lot about children and their needs.

The caregiver handles discipline matters easily without being harsh.

My child likes the caregiver.

My caregiver is supportive of me as a parent.

There are a lot of creative activities going on.

It's an interesting place for my child.

My caregiver is happy to see my child.

For the study, the flexibility experienced by parents was measured in three scales: Work Flexibility, Family Flexibility, and Caregiver Flexibility. We asked some 20 questions about "the flexibility you have in your situation from work, family, and caregiver." Listed below are the statements we used to measure flexibility, parents responding *Never, Rarely, Sometimes, Often,* or *Always.* The flexibility items created three separate scales, the reliability of each of which was measured for internal consistency by calculating a Coefficient Alpha.

Work Flexibility (5 items, Alpha =.74), or the extent to which parents view their job and workplace as a source of flexibility for them, taking into consideration the demands of the job, a workable schedule, allowed time loss or latitude to handle emergencies, a supportive supervisor and organizational climate:

> *Our work schedule keeps changing. (-)*[8]
> *My shift and work schedule cause extra stress for me and my child.*
> *Where I work it's difficult to deal with childcare problems during working hours. (-)*
> *My life is hectic. (-)*
> *I find it difficult to balance work and family. (-)*

Family Flexibility (4 items, Alpha=.78), or the extent to which parents view family members or others within the household as providing them flexibility by sharing responsibilities for child rearing, managing childcare arrangements, and other aspects of family life:

> *I have someone I can share home and care responsibilities with.*
> *In your family, who takes responsibility for childcare arrangements?*
>   *1. I do completely.*
>   *2. Mostly I do.*
>   *3. Equally shared with spouse or other.*
>   *4. Mostly spouse or other does.*
>   *5. Spouse or other does completely.*
> *Do you have a spouse or partner who is employed?*
>   *1. No spouse or partner.*
>   *2. Spouse or partner employed full time.*
>   *3. Spouse or partner employed part time.*
>   *4. Spouse not employed.*
> *I'm on my own in raising my child. (-)*

---

[8] Negatively phrased items require a sign change to create a positive scale.

Caregiver Flexibility (4 items, Alpha=.81) or the extent to which parents have childcare providers on whom they can rely, who will accommodate work schedules and the hours of care needed, be there for emergencies, and understand their circumstances:

> *My caregiver understands my job and what goes on for me at work.*
> *My caregiver is willing to work with me about my schedule.*
> *I rely on my caregiver to be flexible about my hours.*
> *I can count on my caregiver when I can't be there.*

All three scales reflect the idea of flexibility, but of different kinds. These three scales were statistically independent of one another—not correlated. If parents didn't have flexibility from one source, they found it from another, if they could. Relatively few parents found flexibility everywhere, and still fewer found it nowhere. But they found it in complementary ways or in alternative ways, a source affording them high flexibility compensating for lack of flexibility in another.

Illustrating these three dimensions of flexibility is a diagram created by economist Christine Ross in describing my concept of flexibility (Levy 2002; Ross 1998). I include it gratefully, with minor modification, in Figure 5.1. Overall flexibility, from lowest to highest, goes from Point A to Point B. Point A in the diagram is the point of zero flexibility on all dimensions: low flexibility in job, family, and childcare. This unfortunate score might go to a poverty-stricken single mother who lives solo, has a demanding job on weekends and evenings, works a difficult shift with irregular hours, and feels stuck with an uncompromising caregiver. Most parents with such low family flexibility would have managed to find an accommodating caregiver or maybe a somewhat better job, as did the family at Point D. The parents at Point C are able to share responsibilities at home within the family, and the mother has a job with a lot of flexibility in a family-friendly company; so she is able to take advantage of a part-day preschool program that adheres to strict hours. Those fortunate parents who enjoy high flexibility on all three dimensions are at Point B.

Overall statistical findings. As stated earlier in Proposition D, the overall findings from multivariate analysis confirmed that the three kinds of flexibility parents reported, taken together, are positively related to the quality of childcare they reported. A variety of multivar-

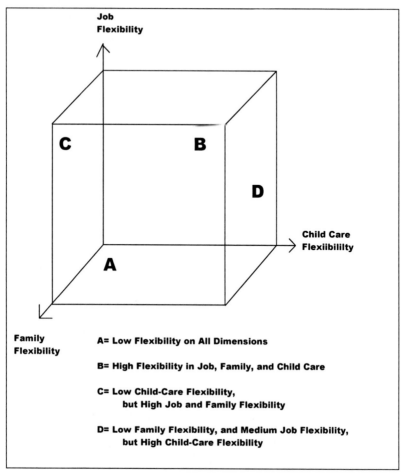

Figure 5.1 Dimensions of Flexibility

iate procedures found flexibility of paramount importance in predicting quality of childcare as measured by the 15-item parent scale (Emlen 1998; Emlen 1999b).

The most obvious finding was that on all regressions of perceived quality of childcare, the sources of flexibility predicted positively, not negatively. This finding contradicts the trade-off hypothesis that parents choose flexibility *instead of* quality.

Among the possible socioeconomic variables entering various predictions of the 15-item quality scale, the sources of flexibility—

work, family, and caregiver flexibility were consistently important, accounting for 18 percent of the variance (R=.42).

A measure of the *accessibility* of childcare was also predictive, and together with flexibility, accounted for 40 percent of the variance of reported quality (R=.63). Being able to find a caregiver "who shares my values" suggests quality of care, as well as whether care could be found in the neighborhood.

Selecting those 606 families using paid market care in centers or family daycare, and examining pairs of quartile groups having lower versus higher quality-of-care scores, logistic regression analysis found the groups most consistently discriminated by accessibility and by work flexibility and caregiver flexibility. The Nagelkerke statistic, which is similar to R squared in a regression, was .59 in discriminating the lowest and highest quartile groups on childcare quality.

As cited above, reported quality of care had no overall relationship to household income—zero correlation—since many aspects of childcare quality are not costly, and the pursuit of income may require "spending" some flexibility. However, household income was significantly associated with family flexibility (r=.46), since those with more resources for flexibility within the family are two-parent families in which both parents may be earners full or part time, or else one of the married parents is enabled to earns a higher income. Household income was inversely with caregiver flexibility (r=-30), since it is the lower-income single parents who are most likely to search for and find greater caregiver flexibility to compensate for their lower family flexibility. These data illustrate why a composite measure of flexibility from multiple sources does a better job of predicting outcomes such as choice of higher quality childcare.

CHAPTER 6

THE FLEXIBILITY SOLUTION

"Parents don't pick their childcare haphazardly or at random.
It must fit with the other pieces of the puzzle."

~The Author

H ere is where measurement of flexibility is really put to
work. Confirming the overall multivariate analysis are two
tables in which the frequencies reveal the dynamics of the
relationship between flexibility and the choice of childcare. The results shown in Table 6.1 support the following—Proposition E: *Each
type of childcare that parents choose fits a different pattern of flexibility and is
part of a distinctive flexibility solution.* Each main type of childcare that
parents chose—care in a center, in family daycare, in the home of a
relative, or in the child's own home with an unrelated caregiver—was
associated with a different pattern of flexibility—a different "flexibility solution." Significantly high, medium or low scores on each of the
three kinds of flexibility, from the three major sources: work, family,
and caregiver, are shown for each type of childcare chosen. The
distinctiveness of each of these flexibility solutions, each one of
which is linked to a different type of childcare, can be appreciated by
reading across the row for each type of care and seeing the pattern of
flexibility involved. "Hi" or "Lo" indicates that the flexibility scores
for that type of care were statistically above or below the mean.[9]
"Av" (average) indicates no significant difference.

What do we find?

---

[9] A t-test comparison with the rest of the sample, N=862.

Table 6.1. Flexibility Pattern by Type of Childcare Chosen

Sources of Flexibility

The Type of Paid Childcare Parents Chose	Work	Family	Care-giver	Hshld Inc.	$s Spent on Care
Centers N=223	Av	Av	Lo	Av	Av
Family daycare N=314	Av	Av	Hi	Lo	Av
Relative's home N=77	Av	Lo	Hi Hi	Lo Lo	Lo Lo
In-home, unrelated N=45	Lo	Av	Hi	Av	Hi Hi ns

- Center care users reported *low* caregiver flexibility, compared with users of relatives, family daycare, and unrelated in-home providers; but center users could take advantage of that resource because they had at least *average* flexibility either from work or from family arrangements.
- Parents who chose care by an unrelated caregiver in a family home—family daycare—reported *high* caregiver flexibility, *average* family flexibility, and *average* work flexibility.
- Parents who used relatives for paid care (grandparents, a relative's home, and all related caregivers in or out of the child's home) reported *average* work flexibility, but *low* family flexibility, since a great many were single parents without other adults with whom they could share home and care responsibilities. They made up for it with *very high* caregiver flexibility. They also had the lowest household incomes and spent the least on monthly childcare expenditures.

• Those parents who had an unrelated person come in to provide in-home care had *low* flexibility from work and *average* family flexibility, but *high* caregiver flexibility. These parents had a wide range of incomes, both high and low, and among the highest child-care expenditures. A number of them had a child with a serious emotional disability, and required extra flexibility from their caregivers.

The importance of these findings is that each type of childcare chosen is associated with its own pattern of flexibility—one of a set of patterns that is distinctive in the way it provides a different solution for use of that type of care. Parents don't just pick out their childcare arrangements haphazardly or at random. Their behavior makes sense. One can see the logic behind it. Parents are adaptive in choosing care that fits their circumstances and meets their needs. They forge a flexibility solution that works—for them.

Examining the results sample by sample. These findings gain validity when we examine the flexibility patterns found in different samples, as shown in Table 6.2. Each sub-sample in the study had special characteristics that either worked for parents or against them, either affording them flexibility or requiring them to seek compensating sources of flexibility. The results support Proposition F: *Different special samples have understandably different patterns of flexibility, further validating the existence of flexibility solutions.* Here are the findings from six samples:

• Recipients of public childcare assistance, who were mostly single parents, reported *very low* family flexibility, but they made up for that by finding flexible caregivers. Even those who used center care had found the most flexible centers.

• An exceptionally high-quality on-site child development center at Mentor Graphics Corporation scored *low* in caregiver flexibility. That was the price of a high-quality program, but the Mentor employees scored *high* in work flexibility and *high* in family flexibility, which enabled those parents to take advantage of that excellent facility.

• Flight attendants working for major airlines faced *very low* work flexibility and reported special difficulty in balancing work and family. Their family flexibility was *average*, but they had *very high* caregiver flexibility. It is hard for these parents to find caregivers with enough flexibility to deal with flight schedules, but they did manage to find them. If they had not mustered enough compensating flexibility, they could not have done that kind of work, and they would not have been in that workforce or in our sample.

Table 6.2. Flexibility Patterns of Special Samples

Sources of Flexibility

Different Samples	Work	Family	Care-giver	Hshld Inc.	$s Spent on Care
Chidcare Assistance (ERDC) N=106	Av	Lo Lo	Hi Hi	Lo Lo	Lo Lo
High-Quality Center (Mentor Graphics) N=72	Hi	Hi Hi	Lo	Hi Hi	Hi Hi
Flight Attendants N=38	Lo Lo	Hi Av	Hi Hi	Hi	Lo ns
Regional Bank (US Bancorp) N=264	Av	Hi	Lo	Hi	Hi
Resource & Referral Service N=74	Av	Av	Hi	Lo	Av
Parents Whose Child Has Emotional or Behavioral Problem N=56	Lo	Lo	Av	Lo	Av

• Parents working for US Bancorp, a regional bank, reported *low* caregiver flexibility, but work flexibility was *average*, and family flexibility was *high*.

• Parents using the services of childcare resource and referral agencies reported *average* flexibility from work and family, but their caregiver flexibility was *high*. Parents who use these services are apt to have more complicated needs and greater than average difficulty finding childcare. They found caregivers who provided them flexibility through this service.

• In a sub-sample of 476 parents of children 3 years or older, 56 parents whose child had an emotional or behavioral problem reported *low* work flexibility and *low* family flexibility, and yet could not adequately compensate for that by finding extra-flexible caregivers. It was not because they didn't try. It was because of their children's extra behavioral difficulties and the challenge that the special childcare needs posed for caregivers. These 56 parents were 20 times more likely than the 420 other parents surveyed to report having had caregivers who quit or let their kids go because of behavioral problems (Emlen 1999a). The challenge faced by the parents in this sub-sample accounts for the fact that they were the only exception, to the general finding that parents compensate for lack of work or family flexibility by finding flexible caregivers. So it should not be surprising that this group of parents paid a price. They reported significantly lower quality of care on all sub-scales measuring childcare quality (Emlen 1999b).

CHAPTER 7

FLEXIBILITY AND QUALITY OF CARE

"The more flexibility they have, the better the quality of
care they are able to find."

~The Author

Now we have seen that the type of childcare parents choose
is embedded in different patterns depending on where they
acquire the flexibility they need. The question is, do those
patterns—those flexibility solutions—have any bearing on the quality
of the childcare arrangements that parents make? Are they choosing
quality, as they define it?

Table 7.1 shows the patterns of flexibility associated with the
overall rating parents gave the care arrangement they had made.

Might the results be biased by quality differences between the
types of care? No. No one type of paid childcare scored better or
worse than another. This lack of correlation of quality with type of
care isn't an original finding (Phillips 1995). But it does apply to our
parent data too. Our parents reported centers of high quality and
low, and the same thing was true for family homes and grandmothers. There is much variation in quality *within* each of the major types
of childcare parents use.

There is, however, a relationship between flexibility and quality
of care, as rated by the parents, after they had responded to all the
specific aspects of the arrangement. This relationship is shown in
Table 7.1:

• The highest reported quality of care came with flexibility from
all three sources: work, family, and caregiver.

• Lower quality came with low flexibility from some sources.

• The lowest quality of care (*fair* or *worse*) came with low flexibility from all sources.

The overall finding is that quality of care, as reported by means of the parent's overall rating, is positively related to a general pattern of greater flexibility—not necessarily to caregiver flexibility, but to flexibility found one way or another. These findings support Proposition G: *Parent ratings of quality of care are linked to patterns of flexibility.*

Table 7.1. Patterns of Flexibility and Parent Ratings of Quality of Care

Flexibility by Source

Parent Ratings of the Quality of Their Childcare	Work	Family	Care-giver	Hshld Inc.	$s Spent on Care
Perfect N=177	Hi	Hi Av	Hi Hi	Av	Av
Excellent N=410	Hi	Av	Av	Hi	Hi
Good N=205	Lo	Av	Lo	Av	Av
Fair N=54	Lo	Lo	Lo	Av	Av
Poor, Bad, or Awful N=8	Lo Lo	Lo Lo	Lo Lo	Lo Lo	Lo ns

Another common suspicion is that parents let what they say about flexibility color or skew how they rate their childcare arrangement. The weight of evidence says that is not the case. It wasn't specifically the *caregiver* flexibility, but an *overall pattern* of flexibility, that related to reported quality of care. We had independent evidence that parents validly discriminated between the quality of the care provided and the flexibility of their circumstances. Parents did not confuse the two issues, even though both are important to them. For example, Mentor Graphics parents using an on-site child development center of exceptional quality reported *high* quality and *low* caregiver flexibility.

They were able to use the Mentor center and take advantage of its high quality but demanding program only because they enjoyed *high* work flexibility and *high* family flexibility. The same pattern was found for a family daycare home known to be providing exceptionally high-quality care, but only on a part-time basis.

For parents to give their childcare arrangement a grade is a weak way to measure quality, but giving a grade or making a "global" rating has a certain face value, and it was correlated with the 15-item scale that measured quality of care solely on the basis of specific items, without mentioning "quality." Mean differences in flexibility were found at each level of rated quality of care. In our independent Kansas City sample, we replicated the chart just shown with similar results.

Now the analysis becomes more powerful. It supports Proposition H: *The quality of care that parents report is related positively to the total net amount of flexibility they have.* Using the reliable 15-item quality-of-care scale and looking at patterns of flexibility, the analysis gives a more realistic picture of the diversity of parents' flexibility solutions and at the same time calculates the total net *amount* of flexibility that parents glean from the different flexibility patterns. This allows us to determine whether the net amount of flexibility gained from any or all sources is related to the likelihood of reporting higher quality of care. This method uses simple frequencies and percentages in a "contingency table." In Table 7.2, combinations of flexibility give the necessary detail, but show the big picture of how they are associated with quality of childcare. The table looks complicated, but it's not, as the reader follows the logic of the table.

Starting with the three columns on the left and bear in mind that we had divided the flexibility scores for each kind of flexibility—family flexibility, work flexibility, caregiver flexibility—into three groups of approximately equal size: *high, middle,* and *low.* The three kinds of flexibility at three levels create 27 possible combinations or patterns of flexibility—ranging from *high-high-high* to *low-low-low* and every combination in between, and shown as dark, gray, or clear.

To analyze the relationships of flexibility to quality of care, the entire table—with the patterns of flexibility—is sorted in ascending order of the percentage of parents reporting quality of care, which appears in the column farthest to the right. The percentages of quality range from 11 percent to 69 percent. This is the percentage of parents in each of the 27 flexibility patterns who reported *low-quality* care. All rows were sorted in order of the percent reporting *low* quality. In the intervening columns, one can examine the frequencies that are the basis for that percentage. All of the quality scores, like the flexibility scores, had been divided into three equal-sized groups of *high*, *middle*, *low*.

Table 7.2 presents a picture of how flexibility is associated with the likelihood of low quality of care. Despite such a diversity of patterns, it is visually obvious that the more consistently parents had a pattern with high flexibility, the less likely they were to report low quality of care (the same results emerged when we analyzed the data by percent of high quality: the scores for high quality dropped from 64 percent for high flexibility to zero percent for the lowest amount of flexibility).

The relationship is linear. It is clearer at the extremes of flexibility than in the middle, but the trend is apparent. Flexibility's relationship to reported quality of care is probabilistic—no iron law of determinism here. Yet despite, or because of, the great diversity of combinations of flexibility, the evidence is clear that, with greater flexibility, parents show a propensity to favor and choose childcare that they assess to be of higher quality.

Table 7.2 is a rich table. It also reveals that it matters less where parents find flexibility than that they do find it somewhere. This finding is confirmed by giving a score to the level of flexibility gained from each source, coding −1 for low, 0 for middle, or +1 for high flexibility. Then, adding those together, each flexibility pattern earns a *net* score that can range from +3 to −3. See the column called Sum Flex.

Then, because the table is divided at the median percent of parents reporting low quality of care, you can compare the sum of the net flexibility scores of all parents reporting either low or high quality care. You can see that net flexibility scores summed to +379 on the patterns of parents least likely to report low quality of care, while the net flexibility scores summed to −255 on patterns of those parents most likely to report low quality of care. That's another way of expressing the strength of the relationship between flexibility and quality.

At the bottom of Table 7.2 is a summary table that emphasizes the linearity of the correlation. The table shows the percent of parents reporting *low* quality of care for each of the net flexibility scores of −3, -2, -1, 0, +1, +2, and +3. The percents are: 69, 55, 43, 34, 24, 18, and 11. That is a very strong correlation, which results from equalizing the sample sizes and compressing the complexity in-between

Table 7.2. Flexibility Patterns in Order of Percent Reporting Low Quality of Care

Flexibility Score, by Source of Flexibility			Quality of Care: Score on 15-Item Scale						
Family	Work	Care-giver	Flex Score	N	Sum Flex	Low	Mid-dle	High	% Low Qual
Hi	Hi	Hi	+3	27	+81	3	14	10	11%
Lo	Hi	Hi	+1	28	+28	4	6	18	14%
Mid	Hi	Mid	+1	36	+36	5	11	20	14%
Hi	Hi	Mid	+2	40	+80	6	15	19	15%
Lo	Mid	Hi	0	36	0	6	15	15	17%
Hi	Mid	Hi	+2	30	+60	6	9	15	20%
Mid	Hi	Hi	+2	34	+68	7	6	21	21%
Mid	Mid	Hi	+1	39	+39	8	17	14	21%
Lo	Lo	Hi	-1	31	-31	8	14	9	26%
Lo	Hi	Lo	-1	22	-22	6	9	7	27%
Hi	Lo	Mid	0	18	0	5	6	7	28%
Hi	Hi	Lo	+1	40	+40	11	14	15	28%
Lo	Hi	Mid	0	21	0	6	9	6	29%
			Σ= +11	402	+379				
Mid	Mid	Mid	0	55	0	16	20	19	29%
Mid	Lo	Hi	0	42	0	13	12	17	31%
Hi	Mid	Mid	+1	51	+51	16	17	18	31%
Hi	Lo	Hi	+1	27	+27	10	10	7	37%
Lo	Mid	Mid	-1	38	-38	15	16	7	39%
Lo	Mid	Lo	-2	26	-52	11	11	4	42%
Mid	Mid	Lo	-1	48	-48	22	17	9	46%
Mid	Hi	Lo	0	15	0	7	7	1	47%
Hi	Mid	Lo	0	47	0	26	13	8	55%
Mid	Lo	Lo	-2	32	-64	19	10	3	59%
Mid	Lo	Mid	-1	24	-24	15	6	3	63%
Lo	Lo	Mid	-2	20	-40	13	5	2	65%
Hi	Lo	Lo	-1	19	-19	13	4	2	68%
Lo	Lo	Lo	-3	16	-48	11	5	0	69%
			Σ= -11	405 862	-255				

Flexibility Score	High or Medium Qual	Low Qual	N	% Low Qual
- 3	5	11	16	69%
- 2	35	43	78	55%
- 1	103	79	182	43%
0	155	79	234	34%
+ 1	167	54	221	24%
+ 2	85	19	104	18%
+ 3	24	3	27	11%
	N=574	N=288	N=862	

the extremes. *Net flexibility* confirms that the relationship between flexibility and quality is linear and strong. Low quality is found with an absence of flexibility, and high quality is found with an abundance of flexibility.

No evidence of a trade-off. The most obvious finding deserves special recognition. The relationship between flexibility and quality is positive, not negative. Parents do not "trade off", i.e., sacrifice, quality for flexibility. For the trade-off hypothesis to find support, the evidence of any correlation would have to be negative, or zero at best—opposite outcomes. But the correlation we found is positive. This research contradicts the trade-off hypothesis.

Why is that important? Because the trade-off hypothesis has reinforced a prevalent attitude that has persisted over the decades and grown more scientific-sounding, as childcare professionals and researchers made a case against parents' motivation and judgment. However, the characterization that parents meet their own needs at the expense of the child's needs turns out to be unwarranted. The behavioral evidence from our research is incompatible with that view. Parents may indeed make a trade-off between many of life's choices. For example, the choice of where to find flexibility may actually be one of those issues where some parents choose one source of flexibility instead of another. But those choices are more on a par—or more neutral—from a values perspective. On the other hand, the evidence regarding quality of care—which is rich in values for parents—is strikingly different. Parents are not sacrificing quality for flexibility—not trading it off. Of course, there are exceptions, and some anecdotal evidence that it can happen; but in the systematic data from many samples, the probabilities say that flexibility makes choice of quality more likely, not less likely.

The most compelling analyses came from examination of the frequencies. They reveal how the choice of different kinds of childcare was associated with different combinations of flexibility— "flexibility solutions"—that in turn were associated with the quality-of-care scores parents reported.

CHAPTER 8

AN EXPLANATORY HYPOTHESIS

"There is nothing so practical as a good theory."

~Kurt Lewin

D rawing conclusions from the evidence presented in the previous chapters, as stated in their several propositions, it is now possible to refute a bankrupt hypothesis and to state an alternative "flexibility hypothesis" that offers a positive understanding of the nature of parental choice of childcare. *Proposition I: The flexibility hypothesis offers a satisfying explanation of how parents make their decisions in choosing childcare.*

Stating an explanatory hypothesis. So, where are we? First, we concluded that the type of childcare parents choose is apt to be part of a distinctive flexibility solution. Each parent's solution probably is unique, but, for each type of childcare, the solutions have similar patterns that are different from those of parents using other forms of childcare. Now we have concluded that—independently of the type of care chosen—in so far as parents acquire flexibility, they are in a position to make what they believe to be better childcare choices from the options realistically available to them. When they can't put together a flexible package, the quality of care suffers. That's what parents are telling us. They find flexibility wherever they can, and as best they can. Flexibility is not only more precious than gold. Parents spend their precious flexibility on choosing better quality of care.

We arrive at a simple but profound conclusion: Parents make the best choices possible—not always, and not necessarily in the ideal world envisioned by their critics or measured by evaluative yardsticks of questionable relevance. In the real world in which they live, however, parents use ingenuity and the resources within reach to craft the best solution they possibly can. And, in doing so, parents demonstrate a propensity to choose quality of care for their children.

We have arrived at a possible theory of flexibility and of choice and of their relationship, which I think provides a satisfying explanation of how parents choose childcare. For a concise statement of the hypothesis and a graphic presentation showing the key concepts and relationships, see Figure 8.1. The concepts are rooted to the corresponding empirical measures that provide the supporting evidence. The hypothesis:

> From the resources available to them, parents create an *optimal flexibility solution* that allows an *optimal choice of childcare*. This choice includes a type of childcare that will *fit* into their flexibility solution and, independently, have a higher *assessed quality of care*.

For a summary of the principal findings on which the hypothesis is based:

1. In order to manage work, family, and childcare with some quality of life, employed parents obtain flexibility mainly from three sources: work arrangements, shared family responsibilities, and reliance on accommodating caregivers.

2. Parents use their sources of flexibility in complementary ways, substituting flexibility from one source to compensate for lack in another, in varied patterns as to which source of flexibility is significantly high or low, or average.

3. Parents do not pick childcare haphazardly or at random. Each type of childcare they choose fits a distinctively different pattern of flexibility—or set of patterns—that works for them.

4. Parents do not sacrifice quality for flexibility; they demonstrate a propensity to choose childcare that they assess as of higher quality, to the extent of the net amount of flexibility overall they are able to corral.

5. Validity issues: Parents can assess detailed and basic aspects of childcare quality with reliability and validity. They discriminate between quality and flexibility, and do not confuse assessments of quality with caregiver flexibility. Perceived quality of care is largely inde-

pendent of age of child, household income, and the types of child-care available to parents. Clear and coherent findings were confirmed and replicated, comparing analyses of data from diverse samples and sub-samples. The theory of flexibility explains parent choice well; however, the data are not longitudinal, and causality is not confirmed.

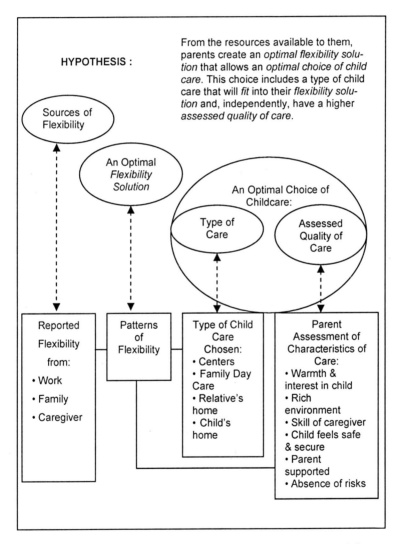

Figure 8.1. Flexibility, Type of Childcare, and Quality of Care

A natural, ecological explanation of parental choice of childcare. Driven by values and shaped by circumstance, parents exhibit a behavioral flexibility that results in successful outcomes. But what kind of behavioral theory is this? Making decisions and ingenuity are psychological behavior, and the sources of flexibility are sociological, involving family, workplace, and relationships in the neighborhood. The choices that parents make have economic consequences for the family, but these aren't just economic decisions. Geographical constraints of time and space shape the solutions and create the need for flexibility. And human values—cultural, family, and personal—account for much of the diversity in the choices made. These choices are best understood as creative ecological behavior.

The theory speaks of an "optimal" flexibility solution and an "optimal" choice of care—in the type of care chosen and in its perceived quality. What does "optimal" mean? To say that parents create an optimal flexibility solution from the resources available to them in their immediate environment, espouses an ecological kind of theory, somewhat analogous to that used in the study of animal behavior. How parents find the flexibility they need, as they pick childcare arrangements, is somewhat akin to the foraging behavior of a hawk that must spend time and expend energy searching for prey. It's a matter of survival whether to stick with the patch where he is or fly to a new patch with fresh pickings. The optimal choice in this trade-off is rewarded by evolutionary survival of the species. When parents choose childcare, they too may stay close to home or go far afield. They too must conserve time and energy. Their success, however, is less fateful than the hawk's, although parents may feel as if successful resolution of a childcare emergency has the urgency of survival. A flexibility crisis can be acutely painful. Why?

For the human animal, success is finding solutions that satisfy a sense of values, particularly regarding characteristics perceived as quality of childcare. In human behavior, values play a significant role in defining successful choice. When the flexibility solution is a fortunate one, quality of care is the reward. Parents apply moral and evaluative standards in making childcare decisions, and optimal choice is the best choice for each parent. It is probably the one that works best for the quality of life of all concerned, child included. And as a result, values help to account for the great diversity in childcare arrangements that work for different families.

The dynamics of parent choice are both value-driven and adaptive. The behavior is creative, and it tends to be successful, within the environmental constraints and with the social resources available. Quality of care means best care feasible, considering the options available. This explanatory hypothesis does not impose an evaluative standard for studying parent behavior—either as the starting point or as the framework. Instead, the behavior is studied within its own context—that is, within the social geography of where and how parents live, work, and find childcare, and as judged by the parents themselves. This is a natural, ecological explanation of parental choice of childcare.

Evidence of a successful market. The evidence also runs contrary to the hypothesis of market failure. Our findings describe more accurately the parent behavior on the demand side of the equation. They reveal use of a highly differentiated supply of care. There is significant diversity in the kinds of care found in the market, and this supply is responsive to variation in parental demand for flexibility and for quality. The evidence reveals *effective demand for quality* as perceived by parents. Parents sought quality and a majority of them found it, many of them in the market. This is not market failure. The alleged evidence that was construed as "market failure" was a largely irrelevant artifact of applying an ideal standard of professional care to the natural conditions of family life.

This is a parsimonious theory of parental choice of childcare. The theoretical value of flexibility lies in its power to explain how parents choose childcare, which choices they make, why they make those choices, and how quality of care enters into that choice. The theory deals rather well with the problem of parent choice of childcare, including choice of quality. Research on this problem has been scattered or too far removed from family life, and generally unproductive of a useful theory of choice. Here, though, is a simple theory worthy of efforts to test, confirm, criticize, or disprove.

It is a parsimonious theory, uncluttered by unnecessary considerations. It doesn't require knowing all of the reasons parents give when asked to reconstruct their decision-making. The theory doesn't necessarily assume a conscious decision-making process, even though the result does have its own logic. Rather, the theory unifies into one coherent set of flexibility variables the underlying significance and impact of a wide range of practicalities that impinge on parent choice and lead to quality. Flexibility emerges as a foundation that *enables* choice of quality care, rather than something for which quality is sacrificed.

Some professional advocates have a predilection for assuming that parent decision-making is conscious, rational, and deliberate, however misguided or ill informed. Perhaps the reason behind this may be to justify efforts to influence, educate, or instruct parents on the finer points of quality of care. Our theory requires no test of knowledge or rationality; it assumes only adaptive and creative behavior. Nevertheless, their choices do make sense, and the findings do focus interest on the possibility that having better options will lead to better outcomes.

The theory is based on data about current use of childcare of different types, and therefore is parsimonious also for not needing to make any assumptions about parent preferences with regard to type of childcare. You cannot logically infer preference from use, nor can you reliably predict use from preference data. But it is more useful to know what people actually do than to know what they might "prefer." Besides, it is difficult to collect reliable data about imagined, and perhaps unfamiliar, alternatives that parents are asked to consider in the abstract, unmindful of how feasibly those alternatives could fit in with family life.

Just as the theory steers clear of the Scylla of preferences, it also avoids the Charybdis of being judgmental about flexibility solutions. How a family creates flexibility may be a stretch that looks impossible to outside observers, involving difficult arrangements, frustrations, or strained relations. However, flexibility is not an exercise of the pleasure principle, and the theory does not assume that flexibility is effortless or painless. I'll cite three examples. An employed mother's use of absenteeism to give her family flexibility when needed may be a source of distress for her. It is not a comfortable form of flexibility for either her or her employer. An employed low-income single mother, having low family flexibility, goes to extraordinary effort to find a flexible caregiver, and that may not be easy, even when the solution is successful. Or consider two-earner couples who stagger shifts, to reduce the total number of hours that both parents work at the same time. They sacrifice time together so one parent can be with the children and so they may avoid the cost of childcare they can ill afford. It requires extra division of labor; they may see less of each other, lose sleep, and feel that the arrangement is a strain. These three examples illustrate that the creation of needed flexibility may appear to have drawbacks. But each different flexibility solution definitely is a solution, and it is likely to be the family's best solution, given the resources at their disposal.

Fallibility. What is the fallibility of the hypothesis drawn from this research? How might it be disproved? Well, there are several possibilities. Although the research compares analyses across varied samples, producing a coherent set of findings that the flexibility theory could explain, nevertheless, each parent's data came from the same moment in time, preventing causal conclusions. Longitudinal or experimental research might clarify the causal relationships and change the picture.

The findings also depend on how variables are defined and measured, and alternative ways of defining variables may produce contrary findings. Actually, flexibility—in concept and theory— is an expandable idea that lends itself to improved measurement. It is likely that more comprehensive measurement of the dimensions of flexibility would strengthen support for the hypothesis. For example, Rosalind Barnett and Karen Gareis at Brandeis University (2006), in studying concerns about unsupervised time after school, examined the effects of parent job flexibility and lengthy commuting time, which were negatively related, and the authors report that "overall, the findings lend support to Emlen's theory" (p. 1395). But other investigators may approach the subject differently. For example, in a study of employed parents' satisfaction with childcare choices, Janis Sabin Elliot (1996) did find trade-offs between satisfaction and competing needs, although satisfaction and perceived quality are not identical concepts.

The effect of sampling can be overriding, too. It is possible that different kinds of parents, living under quite different circumstances, may behave in opposite ways. For example, two friends of mine, who used to be state childcare administrators, point out that when they close down sub-standard childcare facilities, parents sometimes protest and defend the care provided. This appears be an example of sacrificing quality for convenience, and hence a possible contradiction of our hypothesis. Those examples, though, were not studied, and we don't really know the circumstances and perceptions of those parents. Still, my critics might be right. It is conceivable that one might find opposite statistical trends in special populations. Our evidence is compelling, but new samples may challenge the theory, and skepticism serves us better than certainty.

Finally, we must note that this investigator brought a point of view to the subject, which certainly influenced how the research problem was framed. However, although these views cannot be said to have determined the findings that led to the favorable conclusion about parental abilities, my interpretation of the findings is that they reveal the dynamics and wisdom of parent decisions about employment and childcare. I like the research because the behavioral lens shifts attention away from futile blame of personal failings towards seeing how circumstances constrain or empower parents. Only then, I think, will it be possible to take a constructive approach to policy.

Postscript. I have appreciated Karl Popper's work in the philosophy of science, history, and an open society. His perspective on research such as mine is apt, and I end this chapter by quoting him:

> ...I think that our theories about...subjective experiences...should be as objective as other theories. And by an objective theory I mean a theory that is arguable, which can be exposed to rational criticism, preferably a theory which can be tested: one which does not merely appeal to our subjective intuitions...(T)here are no uninterpreted visual sense data...In this sense, an objective theory of subjective perception may be constructed. It will be a biological theory which describes normal perception not as the subjective source or the subjective epistemological basis of our subjective knowledge, but rather as an objective achievement of the organism by which the organism solves certain problems of adaptation. And these problems may, conjecturally, be specified.

> ~Karl Popper, *Unended Quest: An Intellectual Autobiography* (London and New York: Routledge Classics, 1992), pp.160-161.

CHAPTER 9

A NEW DIRECTION IN PUBLIC POLICY

"The essence of life is infinitely and mysteriously multiform, and therefore it cannot be contained or planned for, in its fullness and variability, by any central intelligence."

~Vaclav Havel, *Summer Meditations*[10]

How do the conclusions reached in this treatise help us in thinking about childcare policy and family policy? One reasonable conclusion is that we can't just try to save the children. Trying to establish a universal system of professional-quality childcare is a futile policy agenda. The reason why it is a truly utopian vision is because it could not possibly be implemented in the real world where parental choice produces family solutions of such vast diversity.

Parental choice in family matters should need no justification, but it does. We are talking about biological parents and adoptive parents, mothers and fathers, stepmothers and stepfathers, spouses and partners—all those who have a legal or designated authority to act in the role of parents and make decisions in behalf of the family. Parents have fundamental rights in family matters—and vital interests, such as in having a voice in the policies that affect them. Yet parents have been followed by a black cloud that has darkened their reputation for competence and undermined public acceptance of their legitimate role as chief puzzle solver for the family. This book should help restore respect for their judgment and fend off advocacy

---

[10] (New York: Alfred A. Knopf, 1992), p. 62, in describing the natural economy. Quoted by John McMillan.

of policies that second-guess parents and try to usurp parental choice in childcare, employment, and family matters.

The vain approach to childcare policy contributed to the stalemate over policy and distracted potential advocates from appreciating that childcare must be built upon the economic strength of family and the world of work. The alternative to putting all the policy eggs in the childcare basket to implement far reaching reforms that could improve the ecology of childcare largely by improving the economic capacity of families and the job flexibility of employed parents. The political climate has not been favorable to families for many decades, but such reforms would be socially and politically feasible to implement, because choices would reside where they belong—with parents.

This book has documented the central importance of flexibility in the choices that parents make, and has provided a theory of parental choice that re-directs our attention to the set of policies that affect choice, asking which policies will create the flexibility needed. This means creating resources to support each piece of the puzzle that parents must solve. It means policy to improve childcare, without presuming that a universal solution can replace choice and diversity in childcare. It means finding ways to support the variety of arrangements to which parents turn. It means policy to improve employee benefits, working conditions, and job-scheduling flexibility at the workplace, without presuming that all employers can do this by themselves, unaided by government. It means the creation of decent part-time jobs with basic benefits, and a variety of leave policies. And it means tax policy to help families build and protect their financial capacity, without presuming that all families should make the same decision about employment and childcare. Such policies will require reforms in family taxes, wages, basic benefits, trade, and local economic development. Instead of a relentless pursuit of cheap labor, it means policies that support neighborhoods and the economic strength of families. It means policies supporting a productive and sustainable workforce that will go hand in hand with healthy and sustainable families.

Changing the political climate will be daunting. The country has been going in the wrong direction for many years. Even before the latest financial collapse and economic hard times, the political climate was allowing destruction of workforces, labor markets, and even communities, as family-wage jobs were replaced by poverty-level jobs. Families lost ground in wages and benefits, and in financial security. A tattered safety net failed to catch many whose family emergencies became catastrophes that could have been prevented. Politicians have been unduly influenced by vested interests, preventing passage of universal health care. And, in a blindly speculative climate, unrestrained pursuit of wealth replaced investment in the common good. A burgeoning financial industry invented hedge funds and other high-risk debt-heavy securities containing bundles of mortgages and obscurely derivative assets. In the collapse, as well as in recent decades, hurt most are the families.

It is hard to comprehend the magnitude of irresponsibility driving recent decades. I am struck by similarity to thirteenth century Florentine behavior described by that insightful moral philosopher Dante Alighieri. In his *Inferno*, Dante had a place in one of the rings of hell for every conceivable variety of greed, usury, fraud, treachery and deception. And he knew nothing about telemarketing or securitizing mortgages or opposition to regulatory curbs on market excess and consumer fraud, or of opposition to promoting the public interest and the common good.

Perhaps a pendulum swing back to a period of social and economic responsibility is overdue. If that does happen, then new policies regarding work, families, and childcare will become part of the change, and the flexibility that parents possess will play a key role. So far, this treatise has documented the efficacy of flexibility in parental behavior, but the task in this chapter is to link that understanding to policy. I'll do that by describing some feasible improvements in the sources of flexibility upon which parents rely, and by showing how those improvements could have the desired effect, such as on the quality of childcare. Further, because the conditions that must be in place to improve flexibility are intertwined, the policies favoring family flexibility will depend on the family's financial flexibility, just as workplace flexibility will depend upon policies favorable to the economic sustainability of companies and other employers. Chapter 9 will concentrate on issues concerning improvement of flexibility in the three areas of *work*, *family* (including family finances), and *childcare*. Under each heading, a case is made in support of a proposition relevant to these issues.

• A proposition about workplace flexibility: *Policies favoring work-schedule flexibility, including the choice of a part-time job, will contribute to improved quality of childcare.*

Sylvia Ann Hewlett and Cornel West, in their book *The War Against Parents: What We Can Do for America's Beleaguered Moms and*

Dads (1998), report a Bill of Rights for Parents and raise concerns about relieving economic pressures on parents. In particular, they also call for solving the "parental time famine." As argued in Chapter 4, time and geography are basic to the necessity for flexibility. Some parents have ways of managing long hours of employment, but, on top of significant responsibilities outside of employment, the job options available to employed parents are at the extremes with respect to demands, quality, and flexibility (Drago 2007; Schor 1991). Largely missing are policies that allow parents to reduce their working hours. Bucking the trend towards long hours, a significant proportion of employed mothers and fathers seek shorter workweeks and shorter days. They do this to gain flexibility and to require shorter periods of non-parental care for their children. Those employees who want shorter hours don't usually have that option under existing employment policies and working conditions. For them the full-time option is too extreme, and this source of inflexibility results in unmanageable choices.

High-quality jobs with flexibility, higher pay, and a cafeteria of better benefits have been desired goals for many years, but fewer hours on the job may be especially relevant to the quality of childcare. Assuming a reasonable amount of federal participation, what are a few relevant policy initiatives regarding the workplace that could result in improved quality of childcare? Support parental leave, which allows delay in starting childcare for infants. Allow "comp" time. Support employee choice of manageable shifts and work schedules. Create more part-time jobs with benefits. Of these, the creation of part-time jobs is especially relevant to the quality of childcare.

Research reported by the NICHD Network (NICHD in press) cites both early entry into childcare and long hours of care as among the predictors of behavioral difficulty and poorer developmental outcomes for children. One way to reduce ill effects of daycare is for parents to start it later and use less of it. As Jay Belsky pointed out in an op-ed piece in *The Wall Street Journal* (2003), these initiatives don't get the attention they deserve. Of course, ill effects can also be reduced by improved quality of childcare programs, but it is also quite conceivable that reduced demand for childcare could further enhance the availability and quality of care for those who are using it. Promoting the option of part-time employment and part-time childcare creates a surprisingly unexplored demand-side initiative that could postpone and reduce use of childcare, improving the childcare experience for those children.

• A proposition about family flexibility: *Policies enhancing the financial flexibility of families will contribute to quality of childcare.*

Many employers claim that they cannot be competitive while providing the benefits required to sustain a workforce or the nation's families, and they may be right. Then our recourse must be equitably to address the survival of employers as well as the survival of employees and their families by taking sufficient public responsibility for basic benefits, including the distribution of the risk for health-care needs. As suggested by policy analysts of the New America Foundation, including (Halstead 2004, 2002) and former director of their Work and Family Program (Halstead 2002; Kornbluh 2004), the answer is to invent policies that de-link basic benefits from the vagaries and vicissitudes of employer capacity. They suggest underwriting those benefits by means of mandatory self-insurance of health care and by means of individual 401(k) retirement savings, both federally subsidized progressively.

It is time to adopt safety nets that are life-saving, family-saving, economy-saving, and that provide families with a reasonable prospect of economic security. The safety-net idea needs improvement. Although the idea of unemployment insurance is already familiar and enjoys wide public support, it needs extension and clarification, and it is only a partial, temporary solution. A safety net needn't be conceived as there only after people fall, far below, as in a high-wire act. It cannot be postponed from time of need, from which there may be no bouncing back, and it cannot be full of holes. The "safety-net" metaphor should be tightened up to include benefits that are more like guardrails on the highway, that prevent collision, prevent falling off the road, or just make the road ahead more visible and navigable. Health coverage, savings accounts, and tax reforms with family-investment tax credits are preventive medicine. They prevent unnecessary loss of employment, catastrophic expense, sudden inability to pay the mortgage, family bankruptcy, and the threat even of destitution, hunger, and despair. If safety nets are part of the fabric of life, they create financial security and become a basis for planning ahead. Just as businesses thrive when they have a predictable economic environment, no less do families. Without it they both are vulnerable to failure.

Tax reform itself would yield a safety net, as well as create equality of opportunity. A framework of safety nets would include fundamental reform of both income and consumption taxes, perhaps along the lines suggested by New America analysts (Halstead and Lind 2002). Favorable tax treatment for the family could be added through refundable tax credits for all families with children, not just for childcare expenditures, so as to be neutral on the critical decision parents make about employment and use of childcare. Similarly, a flat, fixed amount of tax credit could be added for those with caregiver expenses for adults with disabilities or frailty. For rent or mortgage payments, instead of deductions that favor wealth and distort the market, why not have a flat amount universally protecting a basic ability to afford housing? Fair taxation will be a critical part of creating supportive family policy. Without legislatively picking preferred solutions that interfere with choice, a rich framework of safety nets will go a long way towards reducing the economic vulnerabilities of families and business alike. That kind of financial flexibility offers families an opportunity to make the choices appropriate for them. For example, a child credit for all families would offer more flexibility than a childcare credit that in effect prescribes a particular choice regarding the amount of employment to seek.

Financial flexibility is missing especially for low-income families, but even two-earner families are not immune. Elizabeth Warren pointed out in *The Two-Parent Trap* (2003) that two-earner families spending all they earn may be at twice the risk of family bankruptcy due to twice the opportunity for a loss of job or health. Many families live paycheck to paycheck, and those receiving public childcare assistance may have to juggle which bill has to be paid next.

Although financial flexibility is an important element in family flexibility, financial flexibility it is not easily achieved by policy initiatives that are shaped by other purposes. This point is illustrated by an admirable, thoughtful experiment with a childcare financing benefit. It illustrates how difficult it can be to appreciate the flexibility needs of parents. A progressive regional bank that had developed a variety of work-family policies including ample support for a counseling and referral service for employees, also offered a financial benefit permitting parents to use pre-tax dollars for childcare. In an employee survey, they discovered that use of that benefit was strongly associated with the employee's household income and that their low-income families did not plan for and use what the bank had thought would be a universally and equitably applicable benefit. The bank responded by investing some of their own dollars into the plan in individual accounts, on a sliding scale, yet still the lower-income employees were unable to use the benefit as much as expected. The plan required employees to anticipate a year's worth of childcare expenses and name a care provider in a tax-reportable transaction. It was a worthy effort to equalize access to a benefit, yet the experiment illustrated how difficult it is to design incentives that really work, and in this case, how difficult it is to overcome the financial insecurity and constraints on planning and choice of childcare that is imposed by low family income.

What should policies about flexibility look like—or not? A telling example of arbitrary denial of flexibility to a powerless social class was reported in the February 14, 2003 edition of *The Wall Street Journal*. The House had just approved a bill that would require mothers on welfare to work 40 hours a week instead of 30, as a condition for collecting benefits. In one stroke, 230 of our national representatives voted to force millions of mothers to increase their use of daycare by 33 percent, overriding whatever flexibility those mothers had crafted as a solution for their precarious effort to become financially independent. It is hard to comprehend the thinking behind such callous and punitive action that would set up a hurdle higher than free single mothers in the wider population try to jump. Families receiving childcare assistance are predominantly young, while other families of employed parents in the population at large, especially of employed single parents, are comparatively older (Emlen 1996). If other parents tend not to enter the labor market until their children are older, then we are already expecting families on welfare to attempt unusual gymnastic feats of management of family, work, and childcare. Adding 10 more hours per week of employment and childcare is adding far more than citizens who are free would choose for themselves or for their children. It could well be much more than the children are able to cope with. It ain't easy when you lose your freedoms!

Another example, reported by the San Diego Union Tribune (Powell 1999), also deals with financial flexibility, but it illustrates how policies that try to second-guess parent decision making can be doomed to miscalculation. County social services gave welfare recipients an Electronic Benefit Transfer or EBT card instead of cash to pay for food, in order to see that children got fed and parents didn't spend their money on cigarettes and soda pop. But with EBT their rent money was coming up short, and a surge in the number of homeless families occurred. EBT was cited as a leading cause. Also noted were family shortages in diapers, baby wipes, toilet paper, shampoo, and toiletries, which the EBT card wouldn't buy. What can we learn from such unanticipated consequences? That when you create policies that try to second-guess parents in managing the budget-making decisions of everyday life or rob them of the flexibility they need to do that, the policy will come back to bite you, as Edward Tenner (1966) says about the revenge of unanticipated consequences.

The financial flexibility provided by public assistance is insufficient. Support for families in need until they are on their own feet does make sense, but in most states the assistance is inadequate. It does not remove the financial instability of having to juggle dire choices and let some bills go unpaid. And it cannot improve future prospects more than marginally, because the policies to improve the economic strength of all families are missing. Karen Tvedt (2009) has documented the wide variation across states in the generosity of state policies, as well as wide differences in the types of childcare supported by different states. It would be plausible to conclude that those differences in parental choices were steered by state policies.

• A proposition regarding childcare flexibility: *Policies respecting parental freedom of choice in childcare are more likely to result in better quality of care than will occur from prescribing choices, whether through the power of subsidies or through the use of quality rating scales.*

Our research supports the proposition that parents place a value on quality of childcare, that they exhibit demand for quality in the childcare market or in their other arrangements not found in organized markets, and that they choose quality when they acquire the needed flexibility in their work schedules, family resources, or supplemental care. Now is the time to put to these findings to the test in the context of childcare policy and in the marketplace. It is important to remember that quality of care does not always require a flexible caregiver, provided that flexibility can be found at home or at work. Quality is sought in its own right. How it is found is another matter.

Does parent demand for quality of care really exist? I believe it does, and I cite a natural experiment where I think it occurred. The child development center at Mentor Graphics Corporation enrolled 25 percent of the company's age-eligible employees in the first year, already high among on-site centers. But over time, as employees learned about how good the program was, enrollment doubled to 50 percent, which is an extraordinary proportion (Browning 2003). They did not switch arrangements and gravitate to the program because it became more flexible. That didn't change; though for convenience some employees moved to live closer. Mentor Graphics parents reported flexibility coming from their work and from their families, not from their childcare program. I believe that over the span of a few years parents' gradual recognition of the program's quality was the lure that accounted for such an extraordinary proportion of individual choices. This childcare program was not competing on the basis of flexibility, but on the basis of quality.

Is it possible that competition on the issue of quality will have similar benefits in the broad childcare market? If so, it may succeed in accomplishing improvements that are difficult to achieve by regulation alone. Regulatory agencies barely have the resources to inspect facilities, and it is an uphill struggle to win conformance with quality standards. The importance of this issue only increases as childcare becomes more of a business, some even provided by for-profit corporations with stockholders. Altruism and professionalism may still dominate as motivations for childcare providers, but profit motives can create a conflict of interest when taking in too many children to care for saves money. It is politically difficult to establish enforceable standards on group size, adult-child ratios, or education and training. On the other hand, informed parents can weigh the relative merits of staff training against the drawbacks of a large group of children. If providers can compete on the basis of such issues, then the market can be a force in the direction of quality. John McMillan's natural history of markets (2002) does not mention childcare, but he discusses using competition to enhance regulatory aims. The idea is applicable, though parents and providers may not be able to exert the essential market force unless a mechanism is established locally (with federal participation in financing) to generate objective, factual indicators of quality for parents to consider.

The regulatory process focuses primarily on minimum standards and the lower end of quality, but here too parents can be engaged. When parents have concerns about childcare that is below some threshold of quality, they have trouble dealing with it, even when they know it is a problem. They need the regulatory system to be their ally. The regulatory agency may feel that it has little time to assist parents in the process, but by shifting some helpful attention to the marketplace relationships between parents and low-quality facilities, agencies may get some leverage they are missing.

An auspice already exists for carrying out an experiment to test the effect of better information on the market. The strategy would be to expand the ability of childcare resource and referral agencies to link supply and demand and help make the market work. Probably at least half the population of parents do not need such a service, but those who do have greater urgency to meet more complicated needs. Throughout the country the resource and referral agency is a community's principal mechanism for facilitating the childcare market by providing unbiased information and helpful counsel to parents, care providers, employers, and the public at large. No other agency or service has that mission. It can support the essentially local, neighborhood character of childcare, but in most communities the funding of existing programs is too anemic for the effort needed. Underfunded, these agencies have not always been in a position to recruit what parents are looking for, nor supply parents with much information about the characteristics of individual providers that could help in assessing quality of care.

With a reasonable investment these services could inject information into the marketplace that would help parents assess quality of childcare facilities, comparatively, and at the same time help providers market the quality of their services on a more factual basis. The idea is not original. Many have stressed the importance of information in the childcare market, and have deliberated on which quality-of-care indicators should be used to provide parents and the community with the information needed (Weber 2003).

In recent years, the idea of using quality indicators in the childcare market has taken hold, though in two divergent approaches. In one, the quality indicators provide hard, descriptive information about the number of children in care together (group size), the ratio of children to adults present, rate of staff turnover, and caregiver education and training. These data are concrete and factual, based on common-sense indicators of quality that have research behind them and that provide information parents may have difficulty learning on their own. Most of the work on developing and using quality indicators has been applied to center care, rather than to care in family homes—though Oregon is implementing such an approach.

Public disclosure of comparative information about individual providers, based on objective indicators related to quality, might well elevate quality as a basis for competition. Providers offering better quality of care could compete with the hype offered by others whose claims of quality are less justified.

The other approach involves the use of five-star ratings of quality. Although star ratings might sound like hotel or restaurant ratings, they are not based on consumer reports or opinion. They are an extension of the tradition of professional ratings of quality. Five stars replace the old evaluative labels, superlative or pejorative, but still wrap the latent descriptive facts in a professional judgment and are subject to the criticisms described in chapter 2. Professional belief in their own evaluative yardsticks has not waned. Many states now implement five-star ratings. See Sue Shellenbarger, "Finding Five-Star Child Care: States Rate Facilities in Effort to Boost Quality," *The Wall Street Journal*, Work & Family Column, March 23, 2006.

Reliance on abstract evaluative ratings, such as the Harms Quality Rating Scale or the five-star approach, may be popular in professional circles, but the factual indicators have more validity. They don't presume to do parents' thinking for them. It remains to be seen whether or not ratings from either approach will encourage providers to compete on the basis of quality or inform parents about critical differences among available providers.

The factual, unbiased information, obtained from surveying providers and maintained by the resource and referral agency on its on-line data files on providers, would be shared with parents requesting information relevant to their choice of care. The information would supplement a parent's own perceptions and judgments. Such information, factual and reliable, could help parents to discriminate between facilities that at first glance seem superficially similar. Perhaps such information could empower consumers, sharpen the search, and create a more informed and accurate demand. If so, it could help redress the imbalance of power parents suffer in the childcare market when the available public information is too abstract and too slanted.

Unfortunately, there seems to be a trend in the direction of using quality ratings. Childcare professionals, state administrators, economists and other analysts, as well as legislators, are venturing down the path of creating and using ideal evaluative standards as a basis for public subsidy, meting out financial rewards and punishments as incentives to both parents and childcare providers in an effort to improve the quality of care provided and to induce parents to use the subsidized care (Weber 2003).

There are several problems with this approach. One, the policy is presumptuous. It denies the existence of parental demand for quality, tries to second-guess parents, and seeks to override their judgment. Two, on the supply side, I think it overestimates the importance of economic incentives, or of extrinsic motivation, as a major factor in the motivation of caregivers. Three, the very concept of *incentive* implies that it works, but begs the question of whether or not it does. Calling something an incentive does not make it one. Four, even assuming that it *will* work, then concentrating demand on a restricted segment of the overall childcare supply is likely to have adverse consequences: If the designated good-quality care is a scarce resource, then stimulating demand to overburden the allegedly better, but scarcely available, supply of care, will be self-defeating. Meanwhile, the narrowly focused effort downgrades support for the more readily available sources of supply, which were a more feasible choice for those parents and perhaps of better quality, as far as anybody really knows.

One encounters many examples of well-meaning initiatives that achieve unanticipated consequences, because of second-guessing parents. Often this is just a case of assuming that *one size fits all,* as when employers settle on a single remedy for the sick-child problem. A company developed a handsome on-site center expressly for the sick child, but many employees didn't want that. So the company developed a program that dispatched caregivers to the child's home, but other parents didn't want an unfamiliar caregiver coming into the home. The company really wanted to be helpful, and underwriting solutions for child illness is probably cost-effective. Yet it doesn't work too well to second-guess parent choice by picking a one-size-fits-all supply-side solution, if no equitable policy is in place. Various demand-side benefits probably would work better, such as subsidizing any kind of backup care that the parents themselves want to establish and prepare a child for. Or such as establishing paid sick-leave as a benefit, coupled with planning for backup at work. Demand-side initiatives do a better job of accommodating the diversity of solutions parents are likely to use.

Another example of a one-size-fits-all initiative has occurred when companies across the land started feeling the urge to offer a childcare benefit. Often the first thing they thought of, frequently because it was lobbied for by a vocal minority of parent employees, was an on-site center. For most companies it was the last thing that made sense, as some discovered. Perhaps, like bank employees, their workforce was distributed into too many neighborhoods. For others, either quality would suffer unless the center was strongly subsidized, or else many parents couldn't afford to use it. But often the biggest surprise was under-enrollment. Many employees wouldn't switch from the arrangements they had, due to preference, transportation and distance, or age complexities within the family. Some on-site centers have been a huge success for those served, but they are relatively rare, and they leave other employees unserved.

Using the *power of the purse* to induce parents to make preferred childcare choices is popular among administrators of public childcare assistance programs. Childcare providers meeting a certain standard of quality receive a higher rate of pay and parents can only receive full subsidy if they use the "quality" care. This is done in the name of "quality of care," although the outcomes are largely unknown. It is said, "We shouldn't be using public money to buy bad care!" Sounds virtuous, but neither should public money be used to discriminate against and unfairly restrict legitimate consumer choices. Regulatory constraints have some legitimacy when designed to protect the public from serious threats to child health and safety or care for too many children at one time. Also reasonable are criminal background checks for offenses such as drug use and physical or sexual abuse, if the findings are relevant to childcare responsibilities.

But what happens when the bar is raised? What happens when the standard for use of public money restricts its use to "good care" based on accreditation, training, or some evaluative rating? Remember that those parents who use relatives or other familiar caregivers exempt from regulation can hardly be said to lack wisdom for not seeking care in a childcare market that has mostly been rated "mediocre or worse." There are other ways more in keeping with a democratic society to bring about improvement in childcare quality, than to place subsidy powers, regulatory powers, and childcare decision-making power all in the same governmental hands. The power to make all those decisions should not be linked. The powers should remain independent.

Accepting the primacy of parental choice as the cornerstone of childcare policy. The diversity of existing childcare arrangement is evidence that a parent's freedom of choice of childcare is de-facto policy already, although it is not honored as a universal principle. Advocates who champion particular choices resist the policy. Yet, not only do parental decisions about employment and childcare represent wide diversity in family circumstances, values, and interests, each decision is likely to result in a wise choice that is the best feasible solution for that family. On the basis of the overall behavioral evidence and for other pragmatic reasons, I am asserting that parents have a legitimate claim to freedom of choice in these family matters. This emerging freedom demands public recognition and protection as a basic liberty, universal for all parents making these choices.

The policy case for parental choice of childcare is central and strong. It alone is in touch with the diversity of demand. Flexibility and freedom of choice go hand-in-hand. One of the virtues of promoting parental choice as a matter of public policy is that it is fine-tuned to meet family needs. It plays out in more variations than planners could possibly imagine. It thrives on diversity and is adaptive, whether we are talking about formal care in the childcare market, informal arrangements, or about the choice of no childcare at all. Success will not flow from second-guessing parents regarding what they want for their children.

To plan and deliver a directed program of childcare, whether legislated or administratively imposed, would be an administrative nightmare. It would be unable to match the diversity of family needs, and it would lack the omniscience to compete with the genius of parental choice. Just because parent choice and market forces have been given a worse name than they deserve, doesn't mean they can be overruled in a democratic society. Managed choice of childcare doesn't have the bad name that *it* deserves, no matter how high the professional quality of the care promoted. It is time to stop going down that road. Karl Popper (1945) liked to say, "The attempt to make heaven on earth invariably produces hell. It leads to intolerance." Respecting the parent's freedom of choice in childcare does require tolerance and discipline. It means not fixating on favorite forms of childcare or single solutions. The road that beckons us has many branches, but it begins with the road sign "Respect parent choice." Then the journey can be more responsive, inclusive, and creative in shaping supportive alternatives. With good information and a few regulatory rules to prevent unsafe and under-staffed care, we can let the market work. This is not some knee-jerk free-market ideology, but a well-grounded case for a well-managed market that allows the greatest amount of choice.

I found an ally in the economist who had made such a strong case for market failure due to lack of parent demand for quality, and I love the irony. David Blau did not use his findings the way his advocate followers did. One of his principles that should guide child-care policy was:

> Child care policy should be based on the presumption that well-informed parents will make good choices about the care of their children. Government can provide the best available information to inform parental decisionmaking and can provide incentives to parents to make good choices for children. But government should not limit the freedom of parents to arrange care for their children as they see fit, subject to caveats about neglect and abuse. Not all parents will want to take advantage of subsidized high-quality child care in preschools and family day care homes. Some will prefer care by a relative or close friend, some will prefer care in a church-based setting that emphasizes religion, and some will prefer a baby-sitter in their own home. These choices may not be optimal from a child development perspective, but government should not coerce parents to raise children in a particular way. As long as safety and general well-being are assured, parents should be the decisionmakers. (2001)

A parent's choice of childcare falls substantially, though not entirely, within the domain of private behavior, even when it concerns care in the childcare market. Like any private choice with public implications, it can't claim a complete right of privacy, but what legitimate authority is better equipped or justified in making those family decisions?

From a political perspective, there are pragmatic reasons for relying on parent choice. Parents can make private decisions that if made by a public agency might be regarded as discriminatory. This is no argument for discrimination, but for avoidance of an inappropriate jurisdiction. Parent choices encompass a host of personal preferences that go beyond the scope of what public policy can address directly. When a parent expresses a preference for "a caregiver who shares my values," that involves cultural, ethnic, religious, and personal subtleties. Public policy, whether in law, rules, or agency practice, cannot easily deal with such preferences. Freedom of choice in such family matters can.

Some of the stickiest issues facing public programs are those related to childcare, and agencies are most vulnerable when they try to influence or control the choices parents make. Many players in society have a legitimate interest in the welfare and development of children, in quality of care, and in other policy goals related to the childcare needs of families. But acknowledging that the primary responsibility rests squarely with parents and families is the only position that works.

For example, how else can it be decided, except within each individual family, how to resolve the gender issues of who works, how much, or which parent will take responsibility for childcare and in what ways? Some parents are feminists, and some are traditional. Some couples draw a sharp division of labor, while others share equally. Culture and personal values shape how that question is resolved. The issue belongs to the family. It is best left as a private matter.

Public policy is best restricted to protecting the freedom of such choices and to crafting policy, such as tax policy, that eliminates discriminatory bias regarding the choices—major or minor. Government attempts to control those family decisions become a legislative quagmire. Localizing the problem to a family level is part of the solution. Government should not be looked to for the choice; only for support of family capacity in decision-making. The answer is to support the process without dictating what the value decisions should be. Government can legitimately make policy to support families, such as a large tax deduction for dependents, but without invading the way families decide to meet their responsibilities.

Childcare choices are indeed an expression of basic values. Parents are not indifferent about their child rearing or their childcare or about having the choice. Freedom of choice in childcare is akin to freedom of religion. The reason we enjoy freedom of religion in this country isn't just because people came here for it. It's because nobody wants anybody else's religion to hold sway over theirs, or wants government to take sides. A truce is called, and tolerance is called for. The standoff assured us freedom of religion, and we established it as a liberty. That principle and the discipline that went with accepting it made democracy possible.

Establishing freedoms and liberties has been a struggle and an evolution. Historian David Hackett Fischer (1989) described how the concept of liberty, and who was entitled to it, differed sharply in each of four early American colonies, Puritan, Quaker, Virginia, and Backcountry. Only the Quakers, invoking the golden rule, believed that freedom of conscience applied to everybody (p. 595-603). If cherished by one's self, then it belonged to others of all religions,

genders, and social classes. Fischer argues that the Quakers' recipro-
cal concept of liberty was absorbed into the national culture and
blended with democratized versions of liberty and freedom from the
other colonies. This belief is part of our culture today, although
many still like to hedge on the exercise of freedom by others.

Herein lies an important liberty for childcare policy as well as for
religion. Childcare policy requires recognizing freedom of choice as a
basic liberty that refuses to allow discriminatory interference with
those family choices. Though strongly but selectively libertarian, such
a policy is not laissez-faire. Rather, it is supported by a strongly progressive policy that improves conditions favorable to family choices.

The concept of *freedom of choice* is fraught with controversy in
many arenas in which values and personal choice are at issue. Some
issues, like abortion and reproductive health, involve life or death
decisions. Freedom of choice must be defined differently in different
arenas where the facts and values differ. The consequences of behavior and the limits of freedom differ for different issues. Assisted
suicide in Oregon requires diagnosis of a terminal condition, a lucid
mind, and consent of two physicians. Abortion choices are defined
by rules regarding age of the fetus and health of the mother, among
other requirements. School choice is constrained by universal educational requirements, and its financing is constrained by rules separat-
ing church and state. Rules about eligibility define who can make a
choice at the ballot box, and impartial rules are supposed to protect
the fairness of eligibility, voting, counting, and announcing the results.

With respect to childcare, freedom of choice is a relatively uncon-
troversial or low-profile issue. Childcare choice can be restrained by
minimum standards regarding criminal records, safety, or numbers of
children per adult, if reasonably applied, and child welfare agencies
have the authority to intervene in instances of child abuse or neglect.
In childcare we are not talking about life or death decisions—perhaps
some unhappiness, health risk, or possible developmental disadvan-
tage. But it is reasonable that childcare should be subject to few mandatory requirements, leaving most issues to parental judgment, supported by improved economic capacity and by better information in
the marketplace. The state has no compelling obligation or authority
to interfere with, undermine, or abridge voluntary use of childcare or
parents' effective freedom to choose childcare.

In sum, freedom of choice, already well-established in existing
parental behavior, deserves to be recognized as the core principle of

a sound childcare policy. It may be our only hope for a compromise on the issues so policy can move forward. I return to my favorite historian for perspective on the tensions over childcare policy and especially over the struggle between freedom of choice and particular choices. David Hackett Fischer has written a richly visual American history of liberty and freedom, ideas which he treats not as abstractions so much as "habits of the heart," a term of Alexis de Tocqueville meaning "customs, beliefs, traditions, and folkways of free people" (2005). Fischer traces their development through wars for freedom and periods of social reform producing new individual liberties, such as universal voting rights and citizenship, civil rights, civil liberties, and egalitarian freedoms. "Through the span of four centuries, every American generation without exception has become more free and has enlarged the meaning of liberty and freedom in one way or another" (p. 722).

Fischer reports on women's suffrage, Rosie the Riveter, and women's liberation, but the emerging freedom of choice in childcare has not been a public issue, and symbols of its diversity have failed to catch the photographer's eye. It may be seen, however, as an extension of the hard-won freedom of women to have choice in occupation and career. It is a relatively short step from there to freedom of choice in matters of childcare, because work and childcare are so interdependent. This next step does not assure gender equality broadly in society or within families where division of labor and shared responsibilities are worked out. Yet it is a crucial step. Only in behalf of family, of whatever composition and in all its diversity in values and circumstances, can parents claim the freedom of choice that is theirs.

Useful knowledge. This book began by drawing the big picture of how parents were managing, and it was a picture of widely diverse family needs and family solutions. Burrowing into the dynamics of how parents make their choices, we discovered their remarkable ability to capitalize on the flexibility available in their immediate environments and to make their best feasible choices of childcare. Then we examined how improvements in that environment at home, at work, and in childcare—through the increased flexibility those improvements might offer—could lead to better outcomes for children than a childcare policy restricted solely to the provision of childcare.

Coming full circle, it is worth asking how much we really know about families, parents, and their children. Especially, how much useful knowledge do communities and states possess about the demographics of families and their needs? That is where the policy and program planning occurs. Often missing, however, are parent voices and parent data about family needs and circumstances, and about their childcare.

One way that parent voices can be heard, individually and in the aggregate, is by seeking parent data through participation in research and by having the findings become part of public discussion. In Oregon, in addition to market-rate surveys of childcare providers and the prices they charge—zip code by zip code—parent data are sought through employee surveys, agency-sponsored consumer surveys, quality-of-care study, and a biennial representative household survey.

Simple facts about families and their children provide information that gives an indispensable demand-side perspective to policy issues. States may know a lot about who is being served by funded programs, but most states cannot tell you how many children are in family daycare homes of various kinds. They have no basis for comparing the lives of those served with those not served. They can't describe the population of all children and all households, analyze the family's marital and employment patterns and child-age factors driving use of paid childcare, or analyze for whom childcare is affordable. Such studies shine a light on the lives of parents so that legislators and administrators don't make policy in the dark. Such studies are no basis for prescribing choice of childcare from on high, but they do provide awareness of diverse needs, and the information can help parents, administrators, and practitioners at the policy table.

A political marriage of childcare policy and family policy. Childcare policy has been caught in a political stalemate of long standing, and neither political party has figured out what to say. Childcare policy is stymied, and for good reason. I have tried to unravel some of the history of this political stalemate. In the briefest terms, it is a history of concern for children, blame for parents, neglect of families, utopian dreams of a sweeping system of professional-quality childcare to save the children, fearful reactions, and a prolonged political stalemate.

For most of a century, while the public blamed mothers for working, and later for staying home, professionals criticized their childcare arrangements, discredited their judgment, and promoted the creation of model facilities as the prescribed alternative. These negative public and professional attitudes have persistently fanned the fires of blame with recurring regularity and little understanding. Researchers joined in and, waving a professional yardstick based on ideal standards, declared that parents were unable to assess the quality of childcare and unwilling to choose it over personal convenience. Alleging lack of demand for quality, the critics blamed parents for a failed childcare market. That parents were unqualified to be competent consumers or decision makers became accepted as a national fact.

The "proven" inability of parents to make wise decisions became justification for designing a professional-quality solution that need not depend on parent choice. It was a subsidized universal solution that would take the place of tax reform, job improvement, or benefit policies that might give parents greater opportunity to make manageable choices about employment and childcare in the real world. Never mind that the professional dream would be impossible to implement in a democratic society. It was inspiring. Motivated mainly by a vision of high-quality childcare, it would create and deliver care by professionally trained staff and produce favorable developmental outcomes for children.

But advocacy of a utopian agenda for a new system of childcare set off alarms, and we've been stymied ever since. Extreme proposals evoke extreme reactions, and advocates on all sides remain poles apart. Free-market devotees see no childcare problem and oppose governmental programs. Anti-daycare forces rail against universal childcare yet are themselves only too willing to do away with parent choice, as long as the legislation prevents maternal employment and commercial daycare. And few would turn existing policy under welfare reform into a general model. Enforcing hours of employment and daycare can only be done to the powerless.

With advocates in a political standoff and no feasible solution in sight, the narrow argument over childcare policy drew attention away from considering other policies that could have been helpful to families. Derogation of parents required saving the children, but not the family. Parents got a bum rap that was used as an excuse for bad policy—bad childcare policy, bad family policy.

I see little chance of a major breakthrough on broad-scale childcare initiatives, but I see some chance of getting wide public support for a more balanced approach including demand-side initiatives that improve childcare indirectly by improving the investment made in the lives of families, employees, the quality of neighborhoods, and the strength of communities. Such reforms are not utopian. They are simply remedies that correct or prevent harmful conditions. They do not try to install idealized institutions requiring a cultural revolution for all to accept. I heed Karl Popper's warnings about attempts to make heaven on earth.

There will, of course, be worthy public discussion of values regarding families, child rearing, child development, education, economic health of families, liberty, and the vitality of markets in accommodating diversity in choices. Nothing can be implemented without the checks and balances familiar to a democratic society. Yet, a viable solution lurks beneath the surface,

Are prospects for a breakthrough really all that bleak? Maybe not. Not if we replace blame with understanding the reasons parents have for making the arrangements they do. Not if evidence of the wisdom of parents' decisions justifies making parental choice in family matters a cornerstone of childcare policy. Not if cultural differences and the value differences between families no longer cause stalemate, because we accept a simple democratic compromise in which each side protects its own values by agreeing not to dictate choices for others. A well-grounded idea in American history, it is but a concept of liberty applied to family matters. And prospects are not bleak if choice occurs within the context of tax policies and safety nets that provide equality of opportunity by evenhandedly supporting all families regardless of which decision parents make about employment, childrearing, and childcare.

Libertarians will back parent choice as a basic liberty deserving of protection; yet, to improve the childcare market, they also might support mechanisms to supply parents with transparent information about providers in the form of descriptive indicators relevant to quality, such as group size and ratio of adults to children. The anti-daycare faction, concerned about families under siege, might well support unbiased tax initiatives supporting the family as an institution. Many parents will look to professionals in early care and education for development of creative ways to improve quality of childcare, if those ways are not packaged as the only subsidized solution for families. The political stalemate will dissolve only when childcare policy reaches beyond exclusive effort to create professional-quality childcare facilities, valuable as they may be.

And we can look to the business community as a natural ally of employed parents. They understand the hard economic fact that, in common with families, their own survival depends on a much-increased public financing of health care and other basic benefits. On the demand-side of the equation, employers understand the diversity of employee choices to be expected in a workforce. They understand the importance of equity. And finally, because they understand that all of the children who someday will be entering the workforce have to come from families.

So it is plausible to believe that we can break the political stalemate over childcare and family support. This treatise made the case for supportive family policies that offer a stronger way to improve the quality of the nation's childcare than is possible from the promotion of childcare alone.

CHAPTER 10

SOLVING THE FLEXIBILITY PUZZLE

T he following is a 2000-word article that was published in the April/May 2008 issue of *Mothers Movement Online*. It is re-printed with the kind permission of the editor Judith Stadt-man Tucker. It summarizes the research reported in this treatise, in a way that highlights the remarkable abilities of parents.

The Mothers Movement Online
www.mothersmovement.org

Solving The Flexibility Puzzle
By Arthur Emlen
MAY 2008

WHEN IT COMES TO JOBS and child care, mothers have the amazing ability to make the best choices possible. And their success depends a lot on how much flexibility they can squeeze from their work schedules, family arrangements, and accommodating child care.

Despite the vigor of the mothers' movement, however, an angry black cloud has continued to follow working mothers, with profes-sional child-care researchers and early-childhood experts raining disparagement on their ability to make wise decisions about child care. As a Portland State University professor emeritus and researcher who has been conducting scholarly studies of families and their child-care choices for more than 40 years, and creating child-care evaluation tools—from a parent's point of view—that are now widely used, I've seen this condescending attitude first-hand.

Does it matter what the public thinks of parents? I think it does. Not only is it hurtful, it's a bum rap used to justify misguided policies, such as creating a universal system of professional child care. This is a utopian dream that has diverted policymakers from addressing the wider range of supports that families desperately need—improved wages, benefits, working conditions, and tax policies, as well as improved neighborhoods and child care.

The conclusion that shines through my research is that parents possess a remarkable ability to make the best choices possible, and they deserve a wider range of options from which to choose. Our research overturns the poor opinion of parents, documents their decision-making ability, and explains the key to their success.

That key can be found in this riddle: What is more precious than gold, but isn't a luxury? The answer: Flexibility! When the subject of flexibility comes up, most of us think only of flexible work arrangements: we need job-sharing, part-time schedules, and the ability to work at home. "If I could only just have a little flexibility on the job," many mothers think, "everything would be OK." And certainly workplace flexibility is important.

But in fact, the need for flexibility is more fundamental. Consciously or not, parents need flexibility on one of at least three fronts to make their work-family juggling act work well—work, family support, or child-care arrangements. It is essential for the success of all the purposeful things you do, and parental employment and child care are no exception. As parents manage the complex demands of work, child care and family life, they are constrained by the physical limits of time and distance, and they absolutely have to arrange flexibility in at least one of these three realms to deal with emergencies and achieve a balance that makes it all possible. At stake are their values and survival itself.

Yet few communities, or companies, or even households are organized to provide working mothers with all the flexibility they need.

I've spent more than 25 years researching how working mothers fit the various puzzle pieces of their lives into a coherent whole that works for them and their family. And what I have learned over the years largely boils down to this: Flexibility, in its many forms, plays an absolutely central role in the lives of employed parents. It's the key for solving the puzzle. Drawing from my research—from many thousands of employee surveys—here are ten big lessons I have learned about flexibility and about how it enables parents to make the best decisions that are possible for them to make:

1. **Flexibility doesn't come out of thin air.** Working parents can't just be flexible—no matter how great their creative abilities—unless they have some flexibility in their immediate environment. Behavioral flexibility depends on having tangible resources that parents can find and draw upon from multiple sources—mainly from their workplace, family, and child care. Of course, there are other potential sources: transportation may be important, and financial flexibility is important for many—although even two incomes do not guarantee flexibility.

2. **Like gold, flexibility is a universal currency.** It may take many forms, but everybody wants it. All institutions compete for flexibility. Workplace flexibility is a prime example—after all, parents are not alone in seeking flexibility. Employers create efficiencies within the business, like just-in-time production, but they also compete strenuously with employees for the flexibility that families can provide. Employers have gradually come to recognize that operating at only their own convenience is not productive, because the flexibility needs of employees are critical and diverse. Flextime, good part-time jobs, and paid leave are major breakthroughs—for those employees who have access to them—and so are the more subtle choices that parents and employers can negotiate for how work is done. The workplace has to provide a big piece of the flexibility puzzle that working parents are trying to solve—and similar logic applies to all employees who have responsibilities for others, young or old.

3. **Even absenteeism is a source of flexibility for employees.** Employee absenteeism takes various forms—lateness, leaving early, interruptions on the job, missed days. Many jobs allow for some amount of absence when an employee's health falters, transportation fails, or her family and child-care (or elder-care) arrangements

break down. Usually the employee makes up for lost time and gets the work done. Employers that try to stamp out absenteeism run the risk of a stressed-out workforce and expensive turnover costs. Nevertheless, absenteeism is generally—and incorrectly—regarded as a problem; most of the time, it should be recognized for its positive contributions. Absenteeism is an informal source of flexibility for employed parents. Furthermore, it is a family solution. The difference between the average absenteeism rates of working mothers (high) and fathers (low) reflects family agreements about which parent will supply the flexibility that makes working feasible for that family.

4. Workplace flexibility is only one piece of the puzzle. The other two large sources of flexibility are family—how working parents divide and share responsibilities at home—and child care—how they make arrangements with accommodating providers of child care. In every community across the land, the types of child care that parents arrange are hugely diverse. Child care can be paid or unpaid, full time or part time, at home or in centers or family homes, by friends, neighbors, nannies, grandmothers or unrelated providers—and in many combinations of these arrangements. That diversity is testimony to the ingenuity of parents, but also to the flexibility that caregivers provide parents. These differences reflect the varied needs of children, as well as the parents' varied work and family resources. All children are different. All family responsibilities are different. *And parents know what they need.*

5. Parents don't pick their child care haphazardly or at random. It must fit with the other puzzle pieces. *All parents discover a "flexibility solution."* And one that uniquely works for them. If the job is severely demanding, a working mom finds most of her flexibility in family arrangements or in child care. Sometimes the child-care service is extraordinary, like when a caregiver accommodates the work schedule of a flight attendant or cares for a child who has a serious emotional or behavioral problem. A single parent who lives solo has relatively little family flexibility and is highly dependent on finding a flexible source of child care. And she does. Sometimes an outstanding child-care program offers little flexibility in its hours and expectations, but parents who have a great deal of flexibility at home and at work are able to take advantage of such a program. It matters less where parents find flexibility than that they do find it.

6. How parents solve their flexibility puzzle isn't always painless. But their solutions make sense. For example, when two working parents stagger shifts so that one parent can be with the children, the arrangement may create some stress. But it is a bona fide solution. Or when a working parent resorts to absenteeism to deal with an emergency, that too is stressful—but it does produce the flexibility needed at that moment. And what is more acutely painful than the moment when you are in a fix, without enough flexibility?

7. Parents care about flexibility, and they care about quality of care. Their pursuit of flexibility is not some selfish preoccupation, in which parents sacrifice quality of care for personal convenience, as some "experts" will tell you. Just the opposite! The quality of the child-care arrangements that parents make depends heavily on how much flexibility they can muster. The quality of care parents want occurs when they have the flexibility they need, and low quality happens when they lack flexibility. The more flexibility they have, the better the quality of care they are able to find. *That* is how parents spend their golden flexibility, and they spend it well.

8. Parents are good at judging the quality of child care. They may or may not be experts in child development, but parents do have a natural ability to size up child care in relation to what their child needs. Parents can judge whether the caregiver likes and accepts their child, and if there is warmth in that relationship. They can tell if Susie or Sam is getting enough individual attention. They are concerned when Maria's day in care is too long. They can see whether too many children are there at one time. They can judge whether the caregiver responds to the children with skill, without resort to harsh discipline. And parents can see if there are lots of interesting things for children to do, What's more, when parents make these judgments discriminating some of the hallmarks of quality of care, they are not confusing quality with flexibility. They know the difference.

9. Parents make the best feasible choices. Most of the time, parents make the best choices they possibly can—not necessarily according to the idealized standards of well-intentioned critics, but according to their own values and what makes common sense, given the resources within their reach. Parents have the values. They have the ability to assess quality of care. They have the ability to make wise choices. They command our respect as the chief puzzle solvers in behalf of families. *And if they have the resources for flexibility, parents make successful decisions.*

10. Flexibility is a policy issue. So a parent's flexibility is a good thing, an essential thing for working families. What can we do to help foster it? Flexibility's fundamental importance points to a new direction in national policy—policy that will create the needed flexibility. What does this mean? It means we create resources to support each piece of the puzzle. It means policy to improve child care, without presuming that universal child care can take the place of diversity in choice of care. It means policy to improve basic benefits, working conditions, and flexibility at the workplace, without presuming that all employers can do this by themselves, unaided by government. And it means tax policy to help families build and protect their financial capacity, without presuming that all families should make the same decision about employment and child care. This will require some reforms in trade and local economic development, in neighborhood development, in taxes, wages, and basic benefits. Instead of a relentless pursuit of cheap labor, we need policies that support the economic strength of families. A productive and sustainable workforce will go hand in hand with healthy and sustainable families, who can afford only as much child care as they need and of the kind they want their children to have.

mmo : april/may 2008

Arthur Emlen is Professor Emeritus at Portland State University in Portland, Oregon, on the faculty of the Graduate School of Social Work where he taught child welfare and research methods. You can read more about his research on child care and parents' need for flexibility here (www.ssw.pdx.edu/focus/emlen).

ACKNOWLEDGMENTS

I have many debts of gratitude, culminating in appreciation for encouragement from publisher Jeff Young, formatting wizardry and copy editing by Alicia Katz Pollock, and the welcome responses of Becky Vorpagel and Pia Divine. Shelley Boots energetically promoted an earlier manuscript, and Peter Weber edited much of it midstream. Christine Ross of Mathematica used my concept of flexibility in her research and depicted its dimensions nicely, and Rosalind Barnett reported encouraging confirmation of my work on flexibility. Bobbie Weber, Lee Kreader, Deana Grobe, and other research colleagues have waited patiently.

At Portland State University's Regional Research Institute for Human Services, I am indebted to two long-time colleagues Katie Schultze and Paul Koren, seasoned researchers from many projects over the years. Paul programmed statistical analyses and managed the data files. Paul also designed my University website. I am deeply appreciative of the help I have received from these long-time friends. Institute director Nancy Koroloff, and then Laurie Powers, graciously gave space, resources, and hospitality to this former director when I turned emeritus. Thanks also to Portland State colleagues Barbara Friesen, Eileen Brennan, Joan Shireman, Kristi Nelson, and Karen Tvedt.

I am recently indebted to Lisa Frack who discovered my university website and drew attention to it in her Portland UrbanMamas blog: Activistas.us. She introduced me to the editor of the online magazine Mothers Movement Online, Judith Stadtman Tucker who published the article "Solving the Flexibility Puzzle" in the April/May 2008 issue. I am grateful for that. This treatise supports that 2000-word article.

Working back, the study of child-care quality from a parent's point of view, of which I was principal investigator, was made possible by a grant to Portland State University from the Child Care Bureau, Administration of Children, Youth, and Families, Administration for Children and Families, U.S. Department of Health and Human Services. It was a project in Wave One of the Oregon Child Care Research Partnership. I had a helpful project officer in Pia Divine, who also encouraged my recent work.

A host of parties contributed financial support: Portland State University, Oregon Child Care Resource and Referral Network, Oregon Department of Employment, and Linn-Benton Community College, AT&T, Families and Work Institute, and the EQUIP project. My thanks to Ellen Galinsky for her early encouragement to measure quality of childcare.

The Oregon Child Care Research Partnership is a diverse group of individuals from universities and agencies around the state who have met monthly as a data group since 1989. They were collaborators in many a project. Among them I especially want to thank Bobbie Weber, who then headed the Department of Family Resources at Linn-Benton Community College. She initiated the statewide data group and became principal investigator of Wave Two of the Oregon Child Care Research Partnership. I have been fortunate to have her intensely interested collaboration throughout the years, as well as of her colleague at Oregon State University, Deana Grobe, who took over doing Oregon's biennial Child Care Market Rate Survey, and is doing a better job than I did.

On various surveys and agency projects, I had support, advice and help from many: at the Oregon Department of Human Resources, from former director Kevin Concannon, at the Adult and Family Services Division, from Alvin Damm, Larry Shadbolt, Jim Neeley, Rosetta Wangerin, Bonnie Chalmers, and Mark Anderson; at the Oregon Employment Department, from Janis Elliot, then Tom Olsen, as Child Care Administrator, and Tom Lynch; from Dan Vizzini, City of Portland; at Oregon Progress Board, from Jeff Tryens, Director, and Tim Houchen, Policy Analyst; at the Oregon Child Care Resource and Referral Network, Claudia Grimm Hedenskög, Program Coordinator, Mary Nemmers, Director (before Mark

Anderson), and Becky Vorpagel, who built the statewide computer network.

For the quality-of-care study, important participation came from the Policy Council on Child Care Quality, co-chairs Luis Ornelas, Madlen Silkwood, and Trish Phetteplace, plus from Bobbie and Claudia. Membership of this statewide community group consisted mostly of parents. They helped in shaping the study questionnaire and in considering the findings. Their role as partners was critical and was the precursor of an organization called Parent Voices. I especially wish to thank the 1,115 parents who took the time to give thoughtful answers to that survey. They were discerning in assessing their child-care arrangements, and the data are a tribute to them.

Many persons helped administer or distribute that survey: Claudia and Bobbie arranged and conducted focus groups for testing the questionnaire and helped draw samples of parents receiving services from the Child Care Resource and Referral Network. Doreen Grove, Vice President at US Bank and veteran of work-family surveys we did together, arranged a statewide sample of US Bank employees. Leslie Faught, President of Working Solutions, Inc. and Toni McCullough of Boeing Aircraft solicited a sample of Boeing. Larry Shadbolt and Alvin Damm of Adult and Family Services distributed the questionnaire to parents receiving child-care assistance in the JOBS and Employment Related Day Care Program (ERDC), and Larry incorporated many of our measures in an AFS consumer survey. Wendy Woods of the Child Care Division of the Employment Department helped to obtain sample of parents of children with emotional problems, and Jo Dennis, Director of Therapeutic Day Care for Children's Institute International in Los Angeles, obtained a sample of parents using agency-supported therapeutic family daycare homes.

Two sample sources were important for the study because they were known examples of outstanding quality of care and gave us an opportunity to test the validity of parent perceptions of the care provided. Special thanks to Margaret Browning, founding director of the Mentor Graphics Corporation's Child Development Center, and to Chris Chenoweth, a family home caregiver in Lake Oswego, for inviting the parents in their programs to participate in the study.

Another sample was important for non-traditional work schedules that required employees to find unusually accommodating care providers. Alyce Desrosiers, a senior flight attendant for Delta Air Lines and San Francisco child therapist with long interest in work-family issues, collaborated with me in conducting and writing a study of flight attendants. We secured the participation of flight attendants who belonged to the Association of Flight Attendants—AFL-CIO and lived in Oregon, thanks to AFA International President Patricia Friend, as well as Mary Converse and Sherrie Mirsky from AFA headquarters, who supported us in combining the quality questionnaire with a study of work, family, and absenteeism issues. Michael Katz, MD donated both time and financial support for the study.

For conducting an important replication in Kansas City with well-managed data collection and a clean data file, I am grateful to Kyle Matchell, Sarah Hendrix, and Carol Scott of the Metropolitan Council on Child Care at the Mid-America Regional Council, and to the resource and referral agencies and parents of the area.

Thanks to Rod Edwards for helping me create and update an internet home page that I used to disseminate instruments, methods, scales and other findings as they unfolded.

The Oregon Child Care Research Partnership is one of several research partnerships. We were part of a national Consortium and met at least twice a year in Washington, DC to discuss our research. I am indebted to these colleagues for their keen interest in our project and their helpful commentary, and to Tony Earls and Maya Carlson of the Harvard School of Public Health for making use of our scales in their longitudinal study of child development in Chicago neighborhoods.

Marty Zaslow of Child Trends, Inc. gave me an opportunity to present and discuss project findings at the April 30-May 1, 1998 conference on NIH campus in Bethesda that she and others of the SEED 2000 consortium of federal agencies organized. The findings in my background paper for that conference are incorporated in chapter 5. I also appreciated exchanges with Chris Ross, economist at Mathematica Policy Research, Inc. who was at that conference and who used the concepts and findings in examining the impact of work, family, and caregiver flexibility on job stability for low-income families. My thanks also to others who early on saw the common sense and importance of flexibility and its relationship to quality, including Gwen Morgan of Wheelock College, Roger Neugebauer of the *Child Care Information Exchange*, and Sue Shellenbarger in her "Work and Family" column in *The Wall Street Journal*.

During the 1980s, my research on work and family issues began with a survey of three Washington, D.C. companies under the auspices of the Greater Washington Research Center (Emlen 1982). Atlee Shidler, president of the center and an old friend, made that survey possible, along with the able assistance of Joan Maxwell. Throughout the 1980s, I carried out a series of employee surveys for employers, and my understanding of flexibility came out of those studies, especially from the 1983 survey of 33 Portland employers that Paul Koren and I reported in *Hard to Find and Difficult to Manage: The Effects of Child Care on the Workplace* (1984). It was supported by grants from the Administration for Children, Youth, and Families and from the Office of Planning and Evaluation, both in the Department of Health and Human Services. Pia Divine-Hawkins and Jerry Silverman were Project Officers. Leslie Faught, Executive director of the Child Care Coordinating Council, negotiated the survey arrangements. Pia later used our data for her dissertation at the Harvard University School of Education, and I served on her committee.

During the 1980s, I benefited from conferences with Dana Friedman and Ellen Galinsky of the Families and Work Institute in New York, and I was honored to have Ellen come to my retirement symposium and make a keynote address. A study done jointly with my Portland State colleagues Margaret Neal, Nancy Chapman, and Berit Ingersoll-Dayton tested hypotheses about employees who try to balance work with caregiving of children, adults, or elders, with Sage the publisher.

Jumping back to the 60s and 70s, I must cite how much my thinking was shaped by the seven-year U. S. Children's Bureau study of neighborhood family daycare. I honor Alice Collins, Eunice Watson, Betty Donoghue, Quentin Clarkson, Rolfe LaForge, and the contributions of many others: Gail LaForge, Joe LeBaron, Paul Bamford, Nancy Whitelaw, Sue O'Keefe, Barbara Burgess, Katie Schultze, Martha Ann Adelsheim, Audrey McCoy, Betty Glaudin, Anita Witt, Fran Ousley, Elizabeth Bergman, Charles Gershenson, Carl Sandoz, and Gordon Hearn.

Professor Henry Maas, of UC Berkeley and the University of British Columbia, taught me to see people's lives in context.

Finally, but most of all, I salute my dear wife and family. Bitsy and the "kids" are now grown, but they certainly will be glad this is all over.

WORKS CITED

Barnett, Rosalind Chait and Karen C. Gareis. 2006. "Antecedents and Correlates of Parental After-School Concern." *American Behavioral Scientist* 49:1382-1399.

Barnett, Rosalind Chait and Karen C. Gareis. 2006. "Antecedents and Correlates of Parental After-School Concern." *American Behavioral Scientist* 49:1382-1399.

Belsky, Jay. 2003. "The Dangers of Day Care." in *The Wall Street Journal*.

Blau, David M. 2001. *The Child Care Problem: An Economic Analysis*. New York: Russell Sage Foundation.

BLS, Bureau of Labor Statistics. 1997. "Workers on Flexible and Shift Schedules." Bureau of Labor Statistics, Washington, DC.

Brandon, Richard N., Erin J. Maher, Jutta M. Joesch, and Sharon Doyle. 2002. "Understanding Family, Friend, and Neighbor Care in Washington State: Developing Appropriate Training and Support." Human Services Policy Center, University of Washington, Seattle.

Brennan, Eileen M., Jennifer R. Bradley, Shane M. Ama, Natalie Cawood. 2003. "Setting the Pace: Model Inclusive Child Care Centers Serving Families of Children with Emotional or Behavioral Challenges." Research and Training Center on Family Support and Children's Mental Health, Portland State University, Portland, OR.

Browning, Margaret. 2003. "Benefits Manager, Mentor Graphics Corp." Pp. Discussion of employee demand for Child Development Center, edited by A. Emlen.

Bureau, Child Care. 2007. "Introduction to Quality Rating Systems." Pp. 2-3 in *Child Care Bulletin*.

Burgess, Thornton W. 1919. *The Burgess Bird Book for Children*. Boston: Little, Brown & Company.

Coser, Lewis A. 1974. *Greedy Institutions: Patterns of Undivided Commitment*. New York: Free Press.

Cryer, Deborah, and Margaret Burchinal. 1997. "Parents as Child Care Consumers." *Early Childhood Research Quarterly* 12:35-58.

Cryer, Deborah Reid. 1994. "Parents as Informed Consumers of Child Care: What Are Their Values? What Do They Know About the Product They Purchase?" Ph.D. diss. Thesis, University of North Carolina at Chapel Hill.

Culbreth, Judson 1997. "Improvisation—Editor's Note." *Working Mother* September 1997.

Desrosiers, Alyce, and Arthur Emlen. 1997. "Airlines, Flight Attendants, and Dependent Care." Regional Research Institute for Human Services, Portland State University, Portland OR.

Drago, Robert Q. 2007. *Striking a Balance: Work, Family, Life.* Boston: Dollars & Sense.

Elliot, Janis Sabin. 1996. "Employed Mothers' Satisfaction with Child Care Choices: Perceptions of Accessibility, Affordability, Quality, and Workplace Flexibility." Ph.D. diss. Thesis, Oregon State University.

Emlen, Arthur, and Elizabeth Prescott. 1992. "Future Policy and Research Needs." in *Family Day Care: Current Research for Informed Public Policy*, edited by D. L. a. A. R. P. Peters. New York: Teachers College Press.

Emlen, Arthur, and Katherine Weit. 1999a. "Quality of Care for Children With a Disability, 1997 conference proceedings." Pp. 84-87 in *Building on family strengths: Research and services in support of children and their families.*, edited by K. J. Exo, Gordon, L.J., Jivanjee, P., & Blankenship, K. Hilton Hotel, Portland, Oregon: Research and Training Center on Family Support and Children's Mental Health, Portland State University.

Emlen, Arthur C. 1998. "From a Parent's Point of View: Flexibility, Income, and Quality of Child Care." in *Child Care in the New Policy Context*. NIH Campus, Bethesda, Maryland.

Emlen, Arthur C. 1970. "Realistic Planning for the Day Care Consumer." Pp. 127-142 in *Social Work Practice, 1970*. New York: Columbia University Press.

—. 1972. "Slogans, Slots, and Slander: The Myth of Day Care Need." *American Journal of Orthopsychiatry* 43:23-35.

—. 1982. "When Parents Are At Work: A Three-Company Survey of How Employed Parents Arrange Child Care." Greater Washington Research Center, Washington, D.C.

—. 1996. "Stage of Family Development: Some Findings with Implications for Self-Sufficiency, Workshop for 8th Annual Policy Symposium,." in *New Findings on Children, Families and Economic Self-Sufficiency," National Association of Child Care Resource and Referral Agencies*. Washington, DC.

—. 1998b. "AFS Provider Study: From Child-Care Providers Serving Parents Who Receive Child-Care Assistance." Regional Research

Institute for Human Services, Portland State University, Portland, OR.

Emlen, Arthur C., and Paul E. Koren. 1984. "Hard to Find and Difficult to Manage: The Effects of Child Care on the Workplace. A Report to Employers." Regional Research Institute for Human Services, Portland State University, Portland, OR.

Emlen, Arthur C., Betty A. Donoghue, and Rolfe LaForge. 1971. *Child Care by Kith: A Study of the Family Day Care Arrangements of Working Mothers and Neighborhood Caregivers.* Corvallis, OR: DCE Books.

Emlen, Arthur C., Paul E. Koren, and Kathryn H. Schultze. 1999b. "From a Parent's Point of View: Measuring the Quality of Child Care. A Final Report." Regional Research Institute for Human Services and the Oregon Child Care Research Partnership, Portland State University, Portland, OR.

—. 2000. "A Packet of Scales for Measuring Quality of Child Care From a Parent's Point of View, With Summary of Method and Findings." Regional Research Institute for Human Services, Portland State University, Portland, OR.

Fischer, David Hackett. 1989. *Albion's Seed: Four British Folkways in America.* New York and Oxford: Oxford University Press.

—. 2005. *Liberty and Freedom.* New York: Oxford University Press.

Friedman, Dana E. 1991. *Linking Work-Family Issues to the Bottom Line.* New York: Conference Board.

Galinsky, Ellen. 1999: 2000. *Ask the Children.* Harper.

Galinsky, Ellen, Carollee Howes, Susan Kontos, and Marybeth Shinn. 1994. *The Study of Children in Family Child Care and Relative Care.* New York: Families and Work Institute.

Halle, Tamara, and Vick, J.E. 2007. "Quality in Early Childhood Care and

Education Settings: A Compendium of Measures ". Washington, D.C.: Child Trends, Inc.

Halstead, Ted. 2004. "The Real State of the Union." New York: A New America Book, Basic Books.

Halstead, Ted, and Michael Lind. 2002. *The Radical Center: The Future of American Politics.* New York: Anchor Books, Random House.

Harms, Thelma, and Richard Clifford. 1980. *Early Childhood Environment Rating Scale (ECERS).* New York: Teachers College Press.

—. 1989. *Family Day Care Rating Scale (FDCERS).* New York: Teachers College Press.

Harms, Thelma, Deborah Cryer, and Richard Clifford. 1990. *Infant-Toddler Environmental Rating Scale (ITERS)*. New York: Teachers College Press.

Helburn, Suzanne W., and Barbara R. Bergmann. 2002. *America's Child Care Problem: The Way Out*. New York: Palgrave for St. Martin's Press.

Helburn, Suzanne W., ed. 1995. "Cost, Quality, and Child Outcomes in Child Care Centers: Technical Report." Department of Economics, Center for Research in Economic and Social Policy, University of Colorado, Denver.

Hewlett, Sylvia Ann, and Cornel West. 1998. *The War Against Parents: What We Can Do For America's Beleaguered Moms and Dads*. Boston: Houghton Mifflin Company.

Isambert-Jamati, Viviane. 1962. "Absenteeism among Women Workers in Industry." *International Labour Review*.248-261.

Kagen, Sharol L., and Nancy E. Cohen. 1997. "Not By Chance: Creating an Early Care and Education System for America's Children. Executive Summary, The Quality 2000 Initiative."

Keyserling, Mary Dubling. 1972. *Windows on Day Care*. New York: National Council of Jewish Women.

Kontos, Susan, Carollee Howes, Marybeth Shinn, and Ellen Galinsky. 1995. *Quality in Family Child Care and Relative Care*. New York: Teachers College Press.

Kornbluh, Karen. 2004. "The Parent Trap." Pp. 92-96 in *The Real State of the Union*, edited by T. Halstead. New York: A New America Book, Basic Books.

Levy, Denise Urias, and Sonya Michel. 2002. "More Can Be Less: Child Care and Welfare Reform in the United States." Pp. 239-263 in *Child Care Policy at the Crossroads: Gender and Welfare State Restructuring*, edited by S. Michel, and Rianne Mahon. New York and London: Routledge.

Low, Seth, and Pearl G. Spindler. 1968. "Child Care Arrangements of Working Mothers." U/S. Government Printing Office, Washington, D.C.

Morris, John R. 1999. "Market Constraints on Child Care Quality." in *Silent Crisis*, edited by S. W. Helburn.

Murchinsky, Paul M. 1977. "Employee Absenteeism: A Review of the Literature." *Journal of Vocational Behavior* 10:316-340.

NICHD, National Institute of Child Health and Human Development, Early Child Care Research Network. 2006. "Does Amount of Time Spent in Child Care Predict Socioemotional Adjustment During the Transition to Kindergarten?" *Child Development*.

—. in press. "Does Amount of Time Spent in Child Care Predict Socioemotional Adjustment During the Transition to Kindergarten?" *Child Development*.

Partnership, Oregon Child Care Research Partnership. 1995; 2000. "Data for Community Planning." Oregon Employment Department, Salem, OR.

Peters, Donald L., and Alan R. Pence. 1992. "Family Day Care: Current Research for Informed Public Policy." New York: Teachers College Press.

Phillips, Deborah A. 1995. "Child Care for Low-Income Families— Summary of Two Workshops." Washington, DC: National Academy Press.

Popper, Karl R. 1945. *The Open Society and Its Enemies*, vol. 2. Princeton: Princeton University Press.

Porwoll, Paul J. 1980. "Employee Absenteeism: A Summary of Research." Educational Research Service, Inc., Arlington, VA.

Powell, Ronald W. 1999. "Rise in homeless families seen." in *San Diego Union Tribune*.

Prescott, Elizabeth, E. Jones, and S. Kritchevsky. 1972. *Day Care As a Child-Rearing Environment, Volume II*. Washington, DC: National Association for the Education of Young Children.

Rosenberg, Bernice, and Pearl G. Spindler. 1969. "Facts about Day Care, Women's Bureau, Department of Labor." Washington, D.C.: US Government Printing Office.

Ross, Christine, and Diane Paulsell. 1998. "Sustaining Employment Among Low-Income Parents: The Problems of Inflexible Jobs, Child Care, and Family Support: A Research Review." Mathematica Policy Research, Inc., Washington, DC.

Sampson, Robert J., Stephen Raudenbush, and Felton Earls. 1997. "Neighborhood Determinants of Child Well Being: Results from the Project on Human Development in Chicago Neighborhoods." *Science* 277:918-924.

Schenet, N. G. 1945. "An Analysis of Absenteeism in One War Plant." *Journal of Applied Psychology* 29:27-39.

Schor, Juliet B. 1991. *The Overworked American: The Unexpected Decline of Leisure*. New York: Basic Books.

Seliger, Susan 1997. "The Improv Mom." *Working Mother Magazine*, September 1997, pp. 34-40.

Smith, Kristin. 1997. "Who's Minding the Kids? Child Care Arrangements: Spring 1997." U S Census Bureau, Survey of Income and Program Participation (SIPP).

Tenner, Edward. 1966. *Why Things Bite Back: Technology and the Revenge of Unanticipated Consequences.* New York: Vintage Books.

Tvedt, Karen L. 2009. "The Child Care Self-Sufficiency Scale: Measuring Child Care Funding and Policy Generosity Across States." Ph.D. Doctoral Dissertation Thesis, Graduate School of Social Work, Portland State University, Portland, Oregon.

Vandell, Deborah Lowe, and Barbara Wolfe. 2001. *Child Care Quality: Does It Matter and Does it Need to be Improved?* Madison: Institute for Research on Poverty, University of Wisconsin.

Warren, Elizabeth, and Amelia Warren Tyagi. 2003. *The Two-Income Trap: Why Middle-Class Mothers and Fathers Are Going Broke.* New York: Basic Books.

Weber, Roberta, and Jerri Wolfe. 2003. "Improving Child Care: Providing Comparative Information on Child Care Facilities to Parents and the Community." Oregon State University, Corvallis, OR.

Zinsser, Caroline. 1991. *Raised in East Urban: Child Care Changes in a Working Class Community.* New York: Teachers College Press.

Zipf, George K. 1949, 1965. *Human Behavior and the Principle of Least Effort.* New York: Hafner.

ABOUT THE AUTHOR

Arthur Emlen is Professor Emeritus at Portland State University in Portland Oregon, on the faculty of the Graduate School of Social Work. He taught child welfare and research methods, and was founding director of the Regional Research Institute for Human Services, which he directed for 17 years. His research in child welfare addressed issues of family permanency, and his childcare research focused on how working parents make their work, family, and childcare arrangements, how they manage, and how they assess the quality of their childcare.

His research was supported mostly by grants and contracts from the United States Children's Bureau, the U.S. Child Care Bureau, surveys for the State of Oregon, and corporate-sponsored employee surveys of more than 50,000 employees at 125 companies and agencies in 25 cities and 13 states.

From the University of California at Los Angeles Emlen received a BA in philosophy and a masters in social welfare, and from Tulane University a Ph.D. in the same field. At UC Berkeley he was a postdoctoral fellow prior to his current position.

Art Emlen and his wife live in Lake Oswego, Oregon. They have three married children and six grandchildren.

LaVergne, TN USA
15 March 2010
175988LV00001B/1/P